BRAIN SPARK

Cool stories about... Strange Places and Important Events!

Michael Harwood, M.D.
& Adrian Hamburger, M.D.

Brain Spark

Website: brainsparkbook.com
Twitter: @brainsparkbook

ISBN: 979-8-9851257-7-1
Copyright ©2022 Michael Harwood M.D. & Adrian Hamburger M.D.

Front/Back Cover Design: Rob Williams
Caricatures/Cover Art: Elidor Kruja
Editing: Faisal Adeel
Logo Design: Olivia85
All rights reserved.

CONTENTS

HOW TO DEVELOP A BRILLIANT MIND! 1
CHICXULUB CRATER 2
VALLEY OF THE KINGS 4
GANGES RIVER 6
POMPEII 8
MOUNT KILIMANJARO 10
TABLE MOUNTAIN (CAPE TOWN, SOUTH AFRICA) 12
KRAKATOA 14
MACHU PICCHU 16
CAPE HORN 19
MOUNT FUJI 21
DEAD SEA 23
ANGKOR WAT 25
ELLIS ISLAND 27
PANAMA CANAL 30
HOOVER DAM 33
THE TSUNAMI OF 2004 35
TIBET 37
CRUSADES 40
THE BATTLE OF AUSTERLITZ 43
TRAIL OF TEARS 46
CALIFORNIA GOLD RUSH 48
THE ABDICATION OF EDWARD VIII 51
THE 1917 RUSSIAN EVOLUTION 54
JIM CROW LAWS 57
ACLU 59
AUSCHWITZ 62

NATO	65
THE KOREAN WAR	68
CUBAN MISSILE CRISIS	72
THE KHMER ROUGE AND POL POT	74
THE SPACE RACE	78
PENTAGON PAPERS	81
STONEWALL RIOTS	84
KENT STATE SHOOTINGS	86
IRAN CONTRA AFFAIR	89
CHERNOBYL	92
THE CHALLENGER	95
BUSH V. GORE	98
2008 FINANCIAL CRISIS	101
ABOUT THE AUTHORS	104
BRAIN SPARK BOOK SERIES	105

HOW TO DEVELOP A BRILLIANT MIND!

Welcome to the third book in our **Brain Spark** series. The first two books focused on famous contemporary historical figures and cultural icons. More and more parents have been reaching out because they want the young growing minds of today to also have a grasp of important historical and geographical concepts, that unfortunately may not be emphasized enough in school.

As parents and physicians, we have made it our focus to expose young and growing adults to important people, concepts, places, and events. Many of these topics come up during adult conversations, during news events, or even online, and the eager mind feels left out.

For optimal memory formation, we suggest that our books are read from front to back, one essay per day. In addition, we recommend you answer the sets of questions associated with each essay, as well as the **Brain Spark** questions, as those reflect on topics that are 1, 3, 7 and 14 days old.

Studies have shown that one of the keys to long-term memory is repeated exposure over short periods of time. This type of memory strategy is known as **spaced repetition.** Therefore, we have staggered these triggering **Brain Spark** questions to review and re-emphasize the key points (so if a question sounds familiar, that is on purpose!).

Important locations are also highlighted in bold. We recommend that, when you come upon each of the highlighted places, you take the time to find them on a world map. Awareness of geographical locations is another important part of developing a broad knowledge base.

Now, let's get started, and feel that Brain Spark!

CHICXULUB CRATER

How do you even pronounce that word? Well, it sounds like *"Chix – aw – loob"!*

About 66 million years ago, there was a sudden **calamitous** event that led to the **extinction** of over 75% of the animal and plant life on earth.

At that time, the earth's climate was very warm. In fact, there was no ice on the ground, and forests were growing close to the North and South Poles! Dinosaurs were roaming the planet. **Paleontologists** were able to figure out that over a very short period of time, almost all life came to an end! This was the end of the **era** of Dinosaurs.

In 1978, a large crater was found in the **Yucatan Peninsula** of **Mexico**. It was named the Chicxulub Crater after the local town of **Chicxulub**. The crater is over 93 miles wide and 12 miles deep! It is estimated that this crater was formed **66 million** years ago when a very large six mile-wide **asteroid** or **comet** struck the earth. This impact generated almost as much energy as 100 million of the biggest nuclear bombs ever tested. To put that in perspective, the largest bomb ever tested was the Soviet **Tsar Bomba**, and that bomb was 1,500 times more powerful than the combined power of the **Hiroshima** and **Nagasaki** bombs used at the end of World War II!

The explosion pushed so much dust into the atmosphere that the skies became dark, and sunlight could barely be seen for years. A lot of plants died because of the lack of sunlight, which in turn led to the death of many animals due to the lack of food. The only large four-legged animals that survived this extinction event were crocodiles and large sea turtles.

While there have been many theories as to what leads to **mass extinction** events, asteroid collisions are felt to be among the more likely. There have been five mass extinction events in the last 500 million years, occurring roughly once every 50 to 120 million years.

Paleontologist: a scientist who studies **fossils** to better understand life millions of years ago on Earth. This is different from an **archeologist**, who studies human remains to better understand the history of human life.

Calamitous: something catastrophic or disastrous.

Extinction: the end of an organism. Typically, the moment of extinction is when the last individual of a species dies.

Era: a long and distinct period of history.

Asteroid: a space rock that orbits the sun, usually between the orbits of Mars and Jupiter. When these space rocks get too close to Earth, they are called **meteors**. Rarely, these meteors can crash through our atmosphere and hit Earth (at which point they are called **meteorites**).

Comet: a piece of space ice that orbits the sun. As it approaches the sun, the ice and dust from the comet will spread behind it, forming what appears to be a "tail."

1. What is the name of the crater believed to be the site of a meteorite that caused the extinction of the dinosaurs?
2. In which country is the Chicxulub Crater located?
3. What is the name of the largest nuclear bomb ever tested?

Brain Spark

VALLEY OF THE KINGS

In **Ancient Egypt**, leaders (**Pharaohs**) and important government officials would be buried in special royal **tombs**. While some of you may be familiar already with the **Great Pyramids of Giza**, a special area along the **Nile River** valley was also dedicated to burying pharaohs.

The **Valley of the Kings** is within the **Necropolis** of Thebes. **Thebes** was the capital of Ancient Egypt. In Greek, necropolis literally means "city of the dead", and refers to a large cemetery built outside of a city.

Although most of the tombs and graves were opened and robbed over the last 2,000 years, the remaining tombs reveal the wealth and splendor of the Egyptian rulers. These tombs also give us a better understanding of how Egyptians viewed the **afterlife**, and how they prepared their rulers to survive and even enjoy the afterlife.

One of the most famous tombs within the Valley of the Kings is the tomb of **Tutankhamun** (who died in 1325 B.C.). It was first discovered in 1922 by **Howard Carter**, and thankfully it hadn't been looted. There were over 5,000 precious artifacts within that tomb including the famous gold face mask of "**King Tut.**"

Statue of King Tutankhamun

Pharaoh: title used to describe the rulers of Egypt. Pharaohs were the supreme leaders of Ancient Egypt; they owned all of the land, enacted laws, and led the armies. Because of how important religion was in daily life, the Pharaoh was seen as a link between the gods and the inhabitants of Egypt, who would worship the Pharaoh as a god-king.

Tomb: a large enclosure for burying or remembering the dead.

Afterlife: a religious concept that there is life after death. The Ancient Egyptians believed that the only way to an afterlife was to be **mummified** and placed in a **sarcophagus** (a type of coffin). The coffin would be inscribed with instructions on how to survive the afterlife, since the deceased would have to deal with threatening beings and traps.

1. In which country is **The Valley of the Kings** located?
2. What word is used as a title for the supreme leaders of Ancient Egypt?
3. What is the name of the capital of Ancient Egypt?

Brain Spark:

1. In what modern country is the Chicxulub Crater found?

GANGES RIVER

One of the most polluted rivers in the world also happens to be one of the most sacred rivers in the **Hindu** religion. The **Ganges River** gets its water from the snowy peaks of the **Himalayan** mountains, and forms into the third largest river system in the world (after the Amazon and Nile rivers). It empties over 38,000 cubic meters per second of water into the **Bay of Bengal**. Just for comparison, an Olympic-sized swimming pool contains 2,500 cubic meters.

In the **Hindu** faith, the Ganges River is considered to be personified by the goddess **Ganga**. She is typically portrayed as an attractive woman, with four arms, sitting on a crocodile. She is worshipped as the goddess of purification and forgiveness. It is believed that bathing in the Ganges at certain periods of the year will provide forgiveness of sins. In fact, many Hindus believe life is incomplete without bathing in the river at least once in their lifetime.

Many Indian cities along the Ganges have "**ghats**" which are long and wide stone steps that lead to the river. They are not only used as access points for bathing, but are also used for funerals, as spreading the cremated ashes in the holy river is considered a path to heaven.

Unfortunately, the Ganges River has become severely polluted, especially in the last 50 years. This is a significant problem since the Ganges provides water to 40% of India's population! The pollution is due to a combination of people dumping untreated human waste, as well as untreated industrial waste from chemical plants, textile mills and slaughterhouses. The water levels of toxic heavy metals like chromium and mercury are many times above safe levels. Many Indians along the river still use the water to bathe, wash their clothes, clean their eating utensils and brush their teeth. These habits have led to the spread of water-borne diseases including **dysentery**, **cholera,** and **hepatitis**. In fact, severe diarrhea is one of the leading causes of death for children in India.

There have been several attempts at cleaning the Ganges River, and there has been some progress over the last few decades, attributed to better education and water treatment plants.

Cholera: a disease, spread by drinking contaminated water, causing severe vomiting and diarrhea.

Hepatitis: inflammation of the liver.

Dysentery: an infection of the intestines causing severe diarrhea.

1. The Ganges River is considered sacred in which religion?
2. The Ganges River empties into what bay?
3. The Ganges River is named after which Hindu goddess?

Brain Spark:

1. In what country is the Valley of the Kings located?

POMPEII

One of the most famous cities in history is now an **archaeological** dig. **Pompeii** was a city on the west coast of **Italy**, near **Naples**, that sadly was buried in 13 to 20 feet of ash by the eruption of a nearby volcano, and remained buried in mystery until the 1700s.

Prior to the eruption, Pompeii was part of a thriving **metropolis**, with lavish homes and theaters. However, in 79 A.D., nearby **Mount Vesuvius** erupted. The explosion was massive, sending a deadly cloud of gas 21 miles into the atmosphere, and releasing 1.5 million tons of hot ash per second. The combination of the hot gases and the rapidly falling ash killed almost everyone in Pompeii that day.

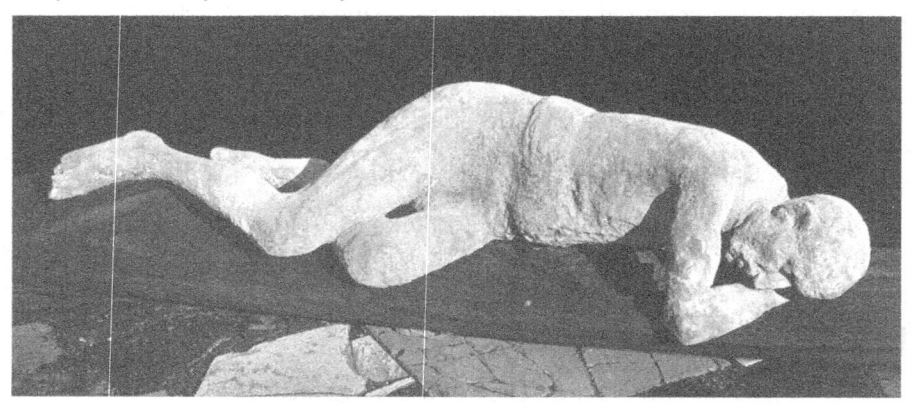

Cast of an older man found at Pompeii

In the 1700s, **excavations** at the site of Pompeii began. Archaeologists found beautiful homes, an amphitheater, and amazingly preserved artifacts of daily Roman life. In the spaces where bodies were buried by ash, plaster was poured to create casts of bodies, so that visitors can observe the shapes of the people whose lives were sadly cut short by the massive explosion. Pompeii is now a tourist attraction, but also a place for further study of the daily lives of ancient Romans.

Strange Places and Important Events

Not too far from Pompeii was the smaller, and much wealthier, town of **Herculaneum**. A large villa, known as the **Villa of the Papyri**, was excavated, and found to be one of the most luxurious Roman villas ever. It had a large collection of amazing sculptures, and more importantly, it housed a large library full of **papyrus** rolls. It is the only surviving library from **antiquity**!

Amphitheater: a theater where the seats create a half a circle, facing a stage.

Artifact: an object made by humans, usually of importance to culture.

Archaeology: the study of human remains to better understand human history and lifestyle.

Metropolis: a large and densely populated city. Pompeii was part of the metropolitan area of Naples, Italy.

Excavation: the careful process of exposing, then digging around remains and artifacts. An excavation site is often called a "**dig**" by archaeologists.

Papyrus: a material similar to thick paper, made out of the stem of the papyrus plant, first used in Ancient Egypt as a writing surface.

Antiquity: a period of history before the Middle Ages, between the 8th century B.C. and the 6th century A.D.

1. Pompeii is located in what European country?
2. What is the name of the volcano that erupted in 79 A.D., covering Pompeii in ash?
3. What is the name of the smaller and wealthier town near Pompeii that was also excavated?

Brain Spark:

1. Which religion considers the Ganges River to be sacred.
2. On what peninsula in Mexico is the Chicxulub Crater found?

MOUNT KILIMANJARO

Did you know that the highest free-standing mountain in the world is in **Africa**? And while you may think of hot weather when you think of the African continent, Mount Kilimanjaro is so tall that it has arctic-like weather at the top, with year-round snow and glaciers!

Mount Kilimanjaro is a **dormant** volcano and is located in **Tanzania** (pronounced *Tan-zuh-nee-uh*). Tanzania is a country in eastern Africa, and is approximately twice the size of California. The peak is named **Uhuru peak**, which means "freedom" in the local language.

Kilimanjaro actually is made up of three volcanic cones. Although the volcano is considered dormant, and two of the cones are extinct (meaning they won't erupt in the future), one of the cones could potentially erupt.

The top of the mountain has been covered by snow for a long time, primarily due to the combination of the high **altitude** (16,100 feet) and freezing temperatures. However, over the last hundred years, the ice cap has shrunk by 85%! At the current rate of warming, it is estimated that all of the ice will be gone by 2060.

The mountain is a very popular tourist destination, and an important source of income for Tanzania. Think twice before climbing the mountain to the top though! Even though it isn't as tall as the mountains of the Himalayan range, getting used to the change in altitude is very hard on the body. It is estimated that about 75% of climbers will experience **Acute Mountain Sickness (AMS)**, due to the combination of high altitudes and low amounts of oxygen. The most severe forms of AMS can be deadly. The best way to avoid getting sick is to go through **acclimatization**. This is a long and **arduous** process that involves sleeping at a certain elevation, climbing up (slowly) for a few hours, then coming down to your previous camp to rest. You would repeat this process for a few days, then move your camp to a higher elevation, and then repeat the process. It can take days or weeks for experienced climbers to adjust.

You would likely recognize this mountain from the **Transformers** movie (it is Megatron's camp), or from Disney's **The Lion King** movie. If you are a book worm, you may recognize it from Ernest Hemingway's short story, **The Snows of Kilimanjaro**.

Dormant: temporarily inactive.

Altitude: the height of an object above sea or ground level.

Arduous: requiring much effort.

Acute Mountain Sickness: an illness caused by climbing to high altitudes. High altitudes have lower oxygen levels, leading climbers to suffer fatigue, headaches, nausea, and shortness of breath.

1. In which country is Mount Kilimanjaro located?
2. What is the name of the peak of Mount Kilimanjaro?
3. What is the name of the Ernest Hemingway short story about Mount Kilimanjaro?

Brain Spark:
1. In what country is the city of Pompeii located?
2. What Greek word means "city of the dead"?

TABLE MOUNTAIN (CAPE TOWN, SOUTH AFRICA)

If you were to visit the city of **Cape Town** in **South Africa**, one of the first things that you would notice is a large mountain behind the city that is almost perfectly flat on top, like a table. So, it makes sense that this mountain is called **Table Mountain**. The top of the mountain is over 3,500 feet tall and is flat for about two miles, with steep cliffs on either side.

Table Mountain as seen from Cape Town (South Africa)

Cape Town is the second largest city in South Africa, and was developed as a port with a **natural harbor** by the **Dutch East India Company**, originally intended as a supply station for Dutch merchant ships traveling to **India** and the rest of **Asia**.

Interestingly, Cape Town was one of the most **racially integrated** cities in South Africa, but after World War II this all changed. **Apartheid** became a racist institution and a political regime in South Africa that pursued **separation** of white people from Black people. Cape Town became very **segregated** with areas only for white people, and Black people were moved to other regions. Black people were even prohibited from working in certain areas.

Strange Places and Important Events

Right outside of Cape Town there is an island called **Robben Island**. This island became famous for its **maximum-security prison** for the white government of South Africa, where political prisoners were held for long periods of time. **Nelson Mandela** is probably the most famous of those prisoners, as he was kept in that prison for 18 years for opposing Apartheid. Once Apartheid ended, Nelson Mandela became the president of South Africa.

Natural harbor: a deeper body of water protected by land that allows the anchoring of boats. The way the land is shaped around a natural harbor typically will lead to protection from strong winds and waves.

Integrate: to allow the mixing of groups or races.

1. Table Mountain is located in which city?
2. Cape Town is located in what country?
3. What is the name of the island famous for its maximum-security prison, used by the white government of South Africa?

<u>**Brain Spark:**</u>

1. In which country is Mount Kilimanjaro located?
2. From what mountain range does the Ganges River get its water?

Brain Spark

KRAKATOA

Did you know that the eruption of **Krakatoa** in 1883 was so loud that it could be heard 3,000 miles away? Did you know that it was so powerful that it burst the <u>eardrums</u> of sailors 40 miles away?

A volcanic eruption darkening the sky

Krakatoa is a volcanic island in **Indonesia**. In 1883, Krakatoa exploded, and was one of the deadliest and most destructive volcanic explosions in recent recorded history. The pressure wave was so powerful that it went around the world four times. The ash from the explosion was pushed 50 miles up into the atmosphere, reaching into space. The eruption also triggered <u>tsunamis</u> that were up to 100 feet high in certain areas.

The explosion destroyed almost the entire island, and pushed so much ash into the atmosphere that the skies around the world were darker for several years. This in turn led to a cooling of the planet for the next few years, with record cold temperatures, blizzards, and snowfalls around the world.

Krakatoa island is part of the **Ring of Fire**. The **Ring of Fire** describes the over 450 volcanoes that form a large circle around the edges of the **Pacific Ocean**.

Tsunami: a very high sea wave triggered by an earthquake, landslide or other large explosion near or in water.

Eardrum: a thin sheet of tissue in your middle ear. It separates the outer ear from the middle ear. It will vibrate with sound, and that vibration gets passed on to tiny bones in the middle ear, which in turn pass the vibration onto the inner ear. The eardrum can get perforated if you insert an object deep into your ear (like a Q-Tip). It can also get torn by a powerful pressure wave. It can be painful when it tears, but in most situations, it can heal on its own over a few weeks.

1. What was the name of the volcanic island that erupted in 1883, triggering 100-foot-high tsunamis?
2. Krakatoa is a volcanic island in which country?
3. What is the term given for the 450 volcanoes that form a circle around the edges of the Pacific Ocean?

Brain Spark:
1. Table Mountain is located in which city?
2. What was the name of the volcano that erupted, burying Pompeii in ash?

MACHU PICCHU

Would you believe that the ancient **Incas** built a fortified royal city on top of a mountain in the 15th century? And that it was close to 8,000 feet above sea-level? This special place is called **Machu Picchu** (the first "c" in Picchu is silent).

The **Incas** created an ancient civilization in **South America**. In fact, they controlled the largest empire in the Americas before the Spanish **conquistadors** showed up. Their empire reached from **Ecuador** into **Chile**, and covered most of the **Andean Mountain range**.

Unlike the **Mayan** civilization, the Incas didn't have a written language. So, almost all of our information about their empire relies on archaeological digs and interpretations.

Machu Picchu

In the **1400s**, the Incan ruler **Pachacutec** built **Machu Picchu** as a royal retreat. Thankfully, the Incas were already used to working and living at high altitude. They also were able to build terraces out of stone and dirt so that they could farm the land on the steep slopes of the mountains.

Machu Picchu was abandoned by the Incas after about a century of living there. It is presumed that they either died because of the **smallpox** virus (introduced by the newly arrived conquistadors), or that they moved away as the Inca Empire was falling apart (also due to the conquistadors).

A Yale lecturer, **Hiram Bingham**, found Machu Picchu while looking for the lost capital city of the Incas. Although at the time, it was fully covered in vegetation and had to be excavated. The process of cleaning up the site took several years.

As the archaeologists uncovered the top of the mountain, they found remarkably preserved stone buildings and walls. They were reminded how the Incas excelled at astronomy, having aligned their temples almost perfectly with specific **constellations** of stars. They also created windows where the sun would shine through on specific days of the year!

Conquistadors: Spanish or Portuguese explorer-soldiers that "conquered" Mexico and South America in the 16th century. Their focus was on gaining territory, and sending treasure (gold) back to mainland Spain and Portugal. While they were responsible for significant exploration, they were also responsible for unintentionally bringing diseases with them and intentionally bringing violence to control the native populations.

Smallpox: a virus that triggers fevers and vomiting, followed by a skin rash. The skin rash then turns into blisters with a dent in the center. The risk of death is about 30%! Those who survived would have scars all over their body, and some would even end up blind. Smallpox has been completely eliminated due to aggressive **vaccination** all over the world. The last naturally occurring case was in 1977.

Constellations: an area in the night sky where a group of bright stars create an outline or pattern, typically of an animal or mythological creature. Some of the more common constellations you may have heard of are Orion and the Big Dipper (also known as Ursa Major).

Maya Civilization: a civilization located in southeastern Mexico and much of what is now Central America. The Mayan people lived in these areas from

2000 B.C. until the final Mayan city was overtaken by Spanish conquistadors in 1697 A.D.

1. What is the name of the fortified royal city of the Incas, built 8,000 feet above sea level?
2. Who found Machu Picchu?
3. What is the word used to describe the Spanish and Portuguese explorer-soldiers who ultimately wiped out native populations in the Americas?

Brain Spark
1. Krakatoa is located in which country?
2. What is the name given to the peak of Mount Kilimanjaro?
3. What is the name of the crater believed to be the site of a meteor that may have caused the extinction of the dinosaurs?

Strange Places and Important Events

CAPE HORN

Easily the most dangerous place on earth to sail a ship is **Cape Horn**. How would you like to go sailing in a place that is usually cloudy or rainy (four to five inches of rain per month), windy (gusts up to 60 miles per hour), cold (average temperature of 41 degrees), and known for **rogue waves** that can reach 90 to 100 feet in height?!

A shipwreck during a storm

In the early days of exploration after Christopher Columbus's discovery of the **New World**, there were many attempts to go from the **Atlantic Ocean** to the **Pacific Ocean** without having to go around Africa. The explorer Ferdinand **Magellan** first discovered a passage to the Pacific Ocean that involved sailing around the southern part of South America in 1520. This passage came to be known as the **Strait of Magellan**.

Unfortunately, the Strait of Magellan is very narrow at some points (only about 2 miles wide) and prone to **williwaws**. Williwaws are sudden, violent gusts of winds that come down from the mountains surrounding the coast. These powerful gusts of winds would hit the sailing ships hard, and drive them into the rocky coasts, leading to many shipwrecks and deaths.

In 1526, a more southern passage to the Pacific was discovered by a Spanish explorer (accidentally, as his boat was pushed south from the Strait of Magellan by a windstorm). This more southern passage came to be called the **Drake Passage**, after **Sir Francis Drake**, who also got pushed south by a storm in 1578.

Cape Horn is a mountainous island at the tip of South America, and is the northern part of the Drake Passage. Over time, this approach around South

America became the preferred way since the Drake Passage was 500 miles wide (and the sailors didn't have to contend with the dangerous williwaws). However, since it is further south, it is prone to far harsher wind and weather conditions.

For the next 350 years, sailors hated that route due to the severity of the weather. It came as a relief when the **Panama Canal** was built in the early 1900s, connecting the Atlantic and the Pacific Ocean through Central America. The Panama Canal has usually very calm winds, and a nice warm tropical climate.

Rogue waves: unusually large and unpredictable waves. It is thought that these are triggered by a combination of high winds and strong currents, when several waves merge to create a large wave. These tall waves can happen in the open ocean, and are sometimes big enough to knock over ships.

1. Cape Horn is located at the southern tip of which continent?
2. What narrow passage through the southern tip of South America was found in 1520?
3. What is the word used to describe sudden, violent gusts of wind coming down from mountains around the coast?

Brain Spark:

1. What empire was responsible for building Machu Picchu?
2. What is the name of the island just outside Cape Town that housed a South African prison?
3. Whose famous tomb was discovered in the Valley of the Kings in 1922?

Strange Places and Important Events

MOUNT FUJI

Easily the most recognizable land feature in Japan is the active **stratovolcano** known as **Mount Fuji**. It is the highest mountain (and volcano) in Japan, measures just over 12,000 feet, and it last erupted in the early 1700s. It is so large that it can be seen from **Tokyo** (62 miles away) on a clear day, and can also be easily identified from the International Space Station!

Mount Fuji has an almost perfect cone shape, and is typically covered in **snow** five months of the year. Its beauty has inspired many famous Japanese paintings and poems. The well-known Japanese artist **Hokusai** created the *One Hundred Views of Mount Fuji* in the 1830s as a three-volume set of illustrations. This set is famous for the iconic ***The Great Wave off Kanagawa*** (with Mount Fuji in the background), which is probably the most recognizable Japanese piece of art in the world.

The Great Wave off Kanagawa by Hokusai
(Mount Fuji is in the background)

Currently, Mount Fuji is a major tourist destination, especially popular among hikers and mountain climbers. It is also a source of national pride and features in many Japanese logos and products. It even inspired the logo of the Japanese car manufacturer, **Infiniti**.

One of the most devastating eruptions of Mt. Fuji is known as the **Hōei eruption**. Although the **Hōei eruption** occurred in 1707, it was preceded by three years of rumblings. The eruption was so powerful that it contributed to the worst ash-fall in Japanese history, releasing over 28 billion cubic feet of ash!

Japan is part of the **Ring of Fire**, a very active volcanic ring around the perimeter of the Pacific Ocean. So many earthquakes and tsunamis hit Japan that they have created special warning systems. The Japanese have also focused on building their homes and skyscrapers to be relatively earthquake resistant.

Stratovolcano: a volcano that produces lava that is stickier and doesn't flow as easily. The layers ("strat" is a Latin-derived word describing layers) of ash and solidified lava form steep slopes around the main vent of the volcano, typically creating a cone shaped structure.

1. Mt. Fuji is located in which country?
2. What famous print by Hokusai is probably the most recognizable piece of Japanese art in the world?
3. What was the name of the 1707 Mt. Fuji eruption that covered much of Japan in ash?

Brain Spark:

1. On which continent will you find Cape Horn?
2. What is the name of the Indonesian island volcano that erupted in 1883?
3. The Ganges River is named after which Hindu goddess?

DEAD SEA

Did you know that if you swim in the water at the lowest point on earth, you will simply float?

The **lowest point** on Earth is on the shore of the **Dead Sea**, at 1,400 feet below sea-level! It is also the deepest salt-water lake in the world (technically it's not a sea, but the name sure sounds cool). It is also the deadliest body of water, because of how salty it is. It is 9.6 times saltier than ocean water! Plants and animals can't survive in that kind of saltiness, hence the name **Dead Sea**.

Interestingly, because of how salty the water is, it changes how humans can swim in the water. Actually, you can't really swim, because the saltiness just makes you float!

Floating bathers in the Dead Sea

Another feature of the Dead Sea is that it spits out small pieces of asphalt (a sticky form of **petroleum**). In the days of Ancient Egypt, it would be used to seal surfaces to protect from water leaks, or for the embalming process of mummies!

The Dead Sea has long been a tourist destination, going back thousands of years. People felt that the salt water, and the special muds around the shore, had healing properties. In fact, one of the first "health" resorts was built by

Herod the Great, the ruler of **Judea**. (You may remember Herod as the ruler who allegedly ordered the Massacre of the Innocents at the time of the birth of Jesus.)

Due to the combination of water evaporation, as well as loss of water inflows due to irrigation needs, the Dead Sea has been slowly shrinking in size. In turn this has also made the Dead Sea saltier. In the last 90 years, the Dead Sea surface area has shrunk by 40 percent! There are talks amongst the local governments to link the Dead Sea to the Red Sea to help replenish its waters.

The Dead Sea is also very rich in minerals, and has been used by **Israel, Jordan, and** the **Palestinian West Bank** as a source of potash (liquid potassium used primarily for fertilization), bromine (used in medications, dyes, insecticides), caustic soda (used in soaps or to unclog drains), magnesium (a light-weight metal), and, of course, salt.

Petroleum: a liquid removed from certain rocks and used to make fuels like gasoline and kerosene.

1. The shores of what sea are the lowest point on Earth?
2. The presence of what mineral causes the Dead Sea to be so dense that people float? (Hint: you put it on your French fries)
3. What biblical ruler built one of the first health resorts at the Dead Sea?

Brain Spark:

1. In which country is Mt. Fuji located?
2. Who found Machu Picchu?
3. What smaller, wealthier town near Pompeii has also been excavated?

ANGKOR WAT

The largest religious complex in the world (more than three times bigger than Vatican City in **Rome**) is located in **Cambodia,** a small country in Southeast Asia. **Angkor Wat** literally means the "**City of Temples**" and houses both a **Hindu** and a **Buddhist** temple complex. In fact, the Hindu temple at Angkor Wat is the largest Hindu temple in the world.

The temple complex was originally built in the 12th century by the ruler of the **Khmer Empire**, dedicated to the Hindu god **Vishnu**. However, by the end of the 12th century it was converted into a Buddhist temple.

The design of the complex involves a long rectangular wall (or enclosure) that is 15 feet tall, and encloses over 200 acres of land and water. Within that wall is a large moat that is over 3 miles around. The central structure is a large temple complex built on a terrace, so that it stands above the neighboring city. There are four large towers at each corner of the central structure, with a very tall tower in the center, reaching over 213 feet.

The towers and structures are covered in religious scenes that have been carved out of the sandstone bricks, with many of the original Hindu scenes replaced by Buddhist designs. In fact, more stones were used to build Angkor Wat than all of the Egyptian pyramids combined!

Although it has been used as a religious destination over the centuries, in the last few decades it has become a major tourist destination, with over 2.6 million visitors in 2018. It was also made famous for the younger, Western generation by its depiction in the video game series (and movie) *Lara Croft: Tomb Raider.*

Vishnu: one of the main gods of the Hindu religion. In Hinduism, Vishnu is the supreme being who creates, protects, and transforms the universe. Typically, statues of Vishnu show a four-armed, well dressed, bejeweled man. Buddhism and Sikhism (both are different religions in Asia) also incorporate concepts of Vishnu within their faiths.

1. In what country is Angkor Wat located?
2. What is the literal meaning of "Angkor Wat"?
3. What two religions have temples housed within the complex of Angkor Wat?

Brain Spark:

1. Which salty body of water is at the lowest point on Earth?
2. What strait near the southern tip of South America, named after an explorer, was discovered in 1520?
3. Ernest Hemingway wrote which short story about Mount Kilimanjaro?

ELLIS ISLAND

Before the **Emergency Quota Act** of 1921, anyone who wanted to move to the **United States** could do so. All they had to do was pack up a few small belongings, have some cash in their pockets, and make their way across the oceans to **immigration processing centers**. The largest center at the time was **Ellis Island**, and it was extremely busy from the 1890s to the 1920s.

Ellis Island is a small harbor island near **New York City** and was initially used in the 1800s as a military fort. By the late 1800s, the government decided to use it as an immigration center due to the large number of people moving to the United States.

Immigrant children at Ellis Island - 1908

At its busiest, Ellis Island would process over 1 million immigrants per year! It is estimated that 40% of current-day Americans can trace their family history through Ellis Island.

Ellis Island was a very busy place. The U.S. government would use inspectors and doctors to evaluate all of the new immigrants. They would look for **physical deformities** (such as a limp, missing arm, eye problems, etc.). They would ask questions to determine if anybody had **mental health problems** (depression, **schizophrenia**, etc.). They would also try to understand who would be unable to work, and therefore become a burden under the care of the government. They would also not allow anyone from **China** or **Japan** to immigrate into the US at the time.

Approximately 1% of immigrants were denied entry into the United States either due to illness, deformities, mental health issues or the inability to work. Those immigrants would be sent back to the countries where they came from. The 99% who passed the inspections would be transferred to ferries and then to trains, where they either met up with family members or found a new hometown for themselves.

So many immigrants came through Ellis Island that the government felt that they needed to limit who could come in even further. They significantly limited people coming from Southern or Eastern Europe. However, professional workers or people from South America were not limited at the time. These European limits reduced the number of immigrants by 80% in the 1920s.

The **Emergency Quota Act of 1921** was a turning point in American immigration. After World War I, there was a growing **anti-immigrant** sentiment in the United States. The government set up for the first time an overall limit on immigration, using a **quota** system to determine those limitations. The quotas used a mathematical calculation to limit people coming from certain countries. It wasn't until the 1960s that the immigration laws were changed to remove this quota system.

After the 1920s, because of the reduced number of immigrants, Ellis Island no longer was needed as an immigration center. It was used as a detention center for prisoners of war during World War II, and then fell into disrepair. It is now open as a museum.

Schizophrenia: a mental disorder wherein people abnormally interpret their emotions and the world, leading to any combination of troubled thoughts, delusions, disorganization, and difficulty in maintaining relationships due to a withdrawal from reality.

Quota: A fixed minimum or maximum number. In this case, quota refers to a fixed maximum number of people allowed to immigrate from certain countries.

1. What was the largest immigration center in the United States from the 1890s to the 1920s?
2. Ellis Island was located near which major US city?
3. What act of 1921 set quotas on how many immigrants could come from certain countries?

Brain Spark:

1. Angkor Wat, the "City of Temples", is located in which country?
2. What devastating eruption of Mt. Fuji occurred in 1707?
3. Cape Town is a city in which African country?

PANAMA CANAL

Ever since explorers and sailors started traveling to the **Pacific** from Europe, there has been a desire to find a quicker (and safer) route from the Atlantic. Prior to the **Panama Canal**, sailors would have to choose the very long route around the African coast and through the Indian Ocean, or they could take the **treacherous** route around Cape Horn (South America).

If only ships could travel between North and South America, the trips would be much safer and faster. **Panama**, a **Central American** country with the shortest distance between the **Atlantic** and **Pacific Ocean,** seemed like a perfect option.

Already by the mid-1500s, the King of Spain had explorers look for a route across Panama, because any advantage in time would strengthen Spanish military and economic might. The engineering at the time just wasn't up to the task.

In the late 1690s, **Scotland** formed a trading company to establish a colony in Panama, and thus control an overland route for goods across its narrow terrain. This was blocked by the English and the Spanish, and the colony collapsed. This was an economic disaster for Scotland, since more than 20% of all Scottish money had been invested at the time in this scheme. (As a side note, this financial collapse led Scotland to finally agreeing to become part of the **United Kingdom** in 1707.)

The French made an intensive effort to dig out a canal in the late 1800s. However, they didn't anticipate how difficult it is to work in an environment with **torrential** rains, venomous snakes and mosquito-borne illnesses like **yellow fever** and **malaria**. Over 22,000 men died working on this project, and the effort failed when they ran out of money and workers.

In the early 1900s, under the guidance of **President Theodore Roosevelt**, the **United States** took over construction of the canal. It took them 10 years to finally complete it, although they ran into many of the same challenges that the French did. The United States eventually handed control of the canal back to Panama in 1999.

The Panama Canal is 51 miles long, and connects the Atlantic to the Pacific Ocean. Because the canal had to be built overland, there are a series of **locks** and artificial lakes, that allow ships to be slowly lifted and then lowered back. Each year, over 14,000 ships make the trip across the canal. It takes about 9 hours for a ship to go from one side to the other.

Large transport ship entering a lock in the Panama Canal

Treacherous: hazardous because of hidden and unpredictable dangers.

Yellow fever: a mosquito-borne viral disease that can cause liver damage, which in turn can cause your skin to turn yellow. This virus is common in Africa and Central/South America, and there is no cure. However, there is a very effective vaccine available which is recommended for anyone traveling to those parts of the world.

Malaria: a mosquito-borne parasite common in Africa, South America and Asia that can also cause severe illness. While there is no vaccine, there are some effective anti-malarial drugs. When properly treated, people can survive this disease. Severe malaria, however, can be deadly. In fact, in 2020, over 600,000 people died from malaria (primarily in Africa).

Locks: short waterways with submerged heavy doors on both ends. When the boat enters a lock, the doors will close, and water is either added or removed. This in turn will either raise or lower the boat, and one of the door locks opens in front of the boat so that it can move to the next body of water. Locks are commonly seen in canals that are connecting bodies of water of different levels.

Torrential: rain that falls rapidly and in large amounts.

1. The Panama Canal connects which two oceans?
2. Which country's failed investment in a trade route through Panama led to it needing to join the United Kingdom?
3. What is the apparatus used in canals involving the addition and subtraction of water in short, enclosed waterways, allowing for the raising and lowering of ships to different sea levels?

Brain Spark:

1. Roughly 40% of Americans can trace their ancestry back to the arrival of immigrants at which famous immigration center?
2. The high amount of what mineral in the Dead Sea allows people to float on the water?
3. Complete the sentence: 450 volcanoes located around the edges of the Pacific Ocean form the Ring of _____.

HOOVER DAM

One of the largest concrete structures built in the 1930s, the **Hoover Dam** is a large dam along the **Colorado River** between **Arizona** and **Nevada**. The goal of the dam was to help control flooding of the Colorado River, help with irrigation of farmland, and to generate electricity (**hydro-electric power**).

It was approved in 1928, and construction began in 1931. This worked out well because this generated many jobs at a time of great unemployment (**The Great Depression**).

The dam is huge. At the base it is 660 feet thick, and at the top it is wide enough (45 feet) to allow for a highway to connect **Arizona** to **Nevada**.

It was a very dangerous work site, with debris falling off the cliff walls from jackhammering or dynamite. Some of the workers figured out that if they dipped their cloth hats in tar, the hats would harden and protect their heads better. These hats worked so well, that the company building the dam made wearing a **hard hat** a safety requirement.

Aerial view of the Hoover Dam

The power generated by the Hoover Dam relies on the pressure of water pushing through **turbines**, thus producing electricity. The dam was the largest hydro-electric power producer in the world at the time of its construction.

Unfortunately, due to increased water consumption throughout the American Southwest, there is less and less water coming down the Colorado River. If the water level drops too much, the dam may not be able to generate any more electricity.

Turbine: a machine for producing power from the flow of water, air or gas past a rotor or wheel

1. The Hoover Dam was built along which US river?
2. The Hoover Dam connects which two US states?
3. In what year did the construction of the Hoover Dam begin?

Brain Spark:
1. In which Central American country was a canal built in order to connect the Atlantic and Pacific Oceans?
2. What Cambodian temple complex's name means "City of Temples"?
3. What is the name of the famous Incan fortified royal city built on a mountain centuries ago?
4. What is the name of the largest nuclear bomb ever tested?

Strange Places and Important Events

THE TSUNAMI OF 2004

Can you imagine that an earthquake can be powerful enough to make the whole Earth shake almost half an inch, shift the earth's spin, and shorten the length of a day by almost seven microseconds?!

On the morning of December 26th, 2004, an undersea **megathrust** earthquake was triggered when a 1,000-mile-long area of rock slipped about 50 feet under the ocean. Long, narrow parts of the seafloor popped up within seconds, generating huge waves on the surface. The amount of energy released by this earthquake was the equivalent of blowing up 1,500 Hiroshima atomic bombs under the water!

The dramatic rise of the seabed triggered a **tsunami**. Tsunami is a Japanese word that means **"harbor wave."** Instead of appearing as a breaking wave, like what you would expect to see on a windy day at the beach, it looks like a rapidly rising tide. Tsunamis are usually a series of large waves that arrive over the course of minutes to hours, called a **"wave train."** While over deep ocean, these waves travel between 300 and 600 miles per hour! As the waves come closer to shore, they slow down to approximately 10 miles per hour, but they significantly increase in height. Some of the waves from the 2004 tsunami were as tall as 100 feet! One of the ways that you can tell that a large tsunami wave is coming is that the ocean will actually pull water away from the beach before the waves start hitting. The best thing to do is to run for the highest ground possible.

The **2004 tsunami** was, as you can imagine, incredibly destructive. The earthquake occurred about 100 miles west of **Indonesia** in the **Indian Ocean**. The first areas to be hit were the **Aceh** province of Indonesia, the island country of **Sri Lanka**, the eastern coast of **India** and the western coasts of Thailand. Over 227,000 people died, 125,000 were injured, and 43,000 went missing.

Due to the catastrophic effects of the 2004 tsunami, the **Pacific Tsunami Warning Center** added more buoys throughout the Pacific Ocean. This allows early detection of tsunamis, which in turn provides for an early warning system for coastlines to evacuate.

Megathrust: a large and powerful earthquake that occurs at a subduction zone, which is an area where one of the earth's tectonic plates is forced under another tectonic plate. These are commonly seen in the Pacific and Indian Ocean.

1. In what year did a major tsunami kill over 227,000 people in Southeast Asia?
2. What word is Japanese for "harbor wave"?
3. In which ocean did the mega thrust earthquake occur that triggered the 2004 tsunami?

Brain Spark:
1. Along which U.S. river is the Hoover Dam located?
2. Ellis Island is located near which eastern U.S. city?
3. What word describes violent gusts of wind coming down from mountains into the coastal sea?
4. Who discovered King Tut's tomb?

Strange Places and Important Events

TIBET

What would come to mind if you heard that a country is the "**roof of the world**"? **Tibet** is a very secluded country (taken over by **Communist China** in 1949) that sits on a very high **plateau** in southwestern China. Tibet has the world's highest capital city (**Lhasa**), the highest road, the highest town, the highest train track, and the highest toilet!

Lhasa - the capital of Tibet

For a long time, Tibet had very few visitors. First, it is at a very high altitude, which means there is 40% less oxygen! Second, it is very hard to get to Tibet since it is bordered by the Himalayan Mountains. Third, China has been restrictive about who can and cannot travel to Tibet.

The history of Tibet is closely linked with the **Buddhist** faith. Although Tibet was at times an empire, a kingdom, or a protectorate of the Mongols, it is best known for being ruled by a **Dalai Lama** from the 1600s until shortly after World War II.

The Dalai Lama is a title given to the spiritual leader of **Tibetan Buddhism**. Tibetans have a strong belief in **reincarnation**, and a search for the Dalai Lama's rebirth starts when the previous Dalai Lama dies. Senior Tibetan monks will check with **oracles** and interpret signs. For example, they will follow the direction of the smoke from the **cremation** of the last Dalai Lama.

The current Dalai Lama (the 14th) was born on a straw mat in a cowshed, to a large farming family. He had to flee China after China took over Tibet. He went into **exile**, and now lives in India. He continues to advocate for more freedom within Tibet. He won the **1989 Nobel Peace Prize** for his work on behalf of Tibet.

On the other hand, China considers the current Dalai Lama to be working against their interests in Tibet. In fact, Chinese authorities kidnapped the 6-year-old re-incarnated **Panchen Lama** (a Tibetan spiritual authority second only to the Dalai Lama) in 1995, and replaced him with a Chinese selected Panchen Lama. The Chinese plan to also select the next Dalai Lama.

The 14th (current) Dalai Lama

The Chinese government has made it clear that it won't tolerate any intervention in its affairs in Tibet, and has gone so far as to make **persona-non-grata** any person who supports Tibet's independence.

Plateau: a large flat elevated piece of land that arises sharply above the surrounding lands.

Reincarnation: the belief that, after death, a soul is reborn into a new body.

Oracle: a person (typically religious) who provides wise predictions about the future.

Cremation: the disposal of a dead person's body by burning it to ashes.

Exile: unable to return to your home country due to political reasons.

Persona-non-grata: Latin term describing someone who is unwelcome.

1. What secluded country located on a plateau in southwest China has been controlled by the Chinese government since 1949?
2. What is the capital of Tibet?
3. What is the name of the spiritual leader of Tibetan Buddhism?

Brain Spark:

1. In what year did a catastrophic tsunami cause great death and destruction in Indonesia, India, Sri Lanka, and Thailand?
2. Which two major bodies of water are connected by the Panama Canal?
3. What Japanese artist created *The Great Wave off Kanagawa?*
4. The Ganges River empties into which Bay?

CRUSADES

The **Prophet Muhammad** is best known for founding the **Islamic Faith**, but what is less well known was his military leadership. By the time of his death (632 **C.E.**), Islamic followers had captured most of current day **Saudi Arabia**. Two years after his death, his followers had captured the Holy Land.

The **Holy Land** is an area that covers modern day **Israel,** the **Palestinian Territories**, **Western Jordan,** and **Southern Syria**. The holiest of cities is **Jerusalem**, which has a special significance to **Jewish** people (their First Temple was built there), **Muslim** people (the Prophet Muhammad reportedly visited Heaven one night in Jerusalem), and **Christian** people (Jesus was crucified just outside of Jerusalem).

By the 11th century, it became a custom in Europe for Christians to travel to Jerusalem as a pilgrimage destination, hoping to have their sins forgiven. **Pope Urban II** initiated the **First Crusade** in 1095 with the goal of recovering the Holy Land from Muslim rule. He promised that anybody who made the pilgrimage to Jerusalem and joined the crusade would receive forgiveness of their sins. Over the next three years, armies of knights and peasants from all over **Western Europe** made their way to the Holy Land.

Eventually they were able to take control of Jerusalem by 1099 and form the **Kingdom of Jerusalem**. This was a time of terrible massacres as the Crusaders would massacre Jewish communities on their way to the Holy Land, and would also massacre the defending Muslims throughout the Holy Land.

In the 1120s, a **Second Crusade** was formed when Christian areas were threatened with reconquest by Muslims. This was the first time that European kings travelled to personally participate in the fights. This crusade failed due to infighting and confusion between the leaders.

In the 1190s, a **Third Crusade** became a long-fought war between English King **Richard the Lionheart** and French King **Philip II** on one side and the **Sultan Saladin** on the other. Saladin was a talented military **tactician** and had already conquered almost all the crusader cities including Jerusalem. The war ended in a truce since both sides had suffered many casualties.

The **Fourth Crusade** started in 1198, but never even made it to Jerusalem. The crusaders did make it to **Constantinople** in 1204, where they ended up looting and burning most of the city (despite it being a Christian city), before ending their crusade.

There were another five crusades throughout the 1200s. They became overall less and less successful, and by the end of the 13th century no further significant efforts were made to reconquer the Holy Land.

C.E.: Common Era, typically used as a replacement for A.D. (Anno Domini) to describe the year. The opposite would be B.C.E (before the Common Era), also known as B.C. (before Christ), which describes the years prior to the birth of Jesus Christ.

Sultan: a Muslim king.

Tactician: a person who uses careful planning and strategy to accomplish a goal.

1. What was the name of the Prophet who founded the religion of Islam (and also was an accomplished military leader)?
2. Which pope launched the First Crusade?
3. Which sultan led the Muslims to battle in the Third Crusade?

Brain Spark:
1. What is the capital of Tibet?
2. Which two states are connected by the Hoover Dam?
3. What biblical ruler built a health resort on the coast of the Dead Sea?
4. What plant was used to make a paper-like writing surface in Ancient Egypt?

Strange Places and Important Events

THE BATTLE OF AUSTERLITZ

The Battle of Austerlitz was one of the most important battles of the 1800s, and is also known as the **Battle of the Three Emperors.** In fact, it is considered one of the best tactical battles of all time.

Napoleon Bonaparte

The French underwent a revolution in 1789, which led to the execution of **King Louis XVI**, and was followed by many years of chaos and terror. Eventually a young military general named Napoleon Bonaparte was able to bring some order to France. Napoleon became a general at the young age of 24 and was so successful in his military career and political leadership that he became the leader of France and, later, **Emperor of the French**.

The rest of the European countries disliked Napoleon. They were unhappy that **Louis XVI** had been **executed**, and that the French were having one military success after another as they expanded their borders.

By 1805, a third **coalition** of powers had arranged themselves to defeat Napoleon. The first two coalitions had failed. The third coalition included **England, Austria, Russia, Sweden, Naples** and **Sicily**.

Napoleon, and his "**Grande Armée**", had seen many successes, and were even able to capture the Austrian army and take control of **Vienna** (the capital city of the Austrian Empire)! The Austrians decided to wait until the Imperial Russian army arrived for a large battle near the town of Austerlitz.

Napoleon chose to play a trick on the Austrians and Russians, sending out signals that his army was weak and in poor shape. This lured the coalition into battle. He purposefully made his right **flank** look weak when the battle started, hoping that the coalition would attack that part of his army first. Little did the coalition realize that another large French army was on its way to attack the coalition as well. This strategy allowed the Grande Armée to destroy large parts of the coalition armies, taking many prisoners.

The Battle of Austerlitz represented a significant defeat for the Austrians, and they had to give up large pieces of territory in Italy and Southern Germany to the French.

However, the Europeans remained enraged by Napoleon's growing power. Within a few months of the end of the **Battle of Austerlitz**, a Fourth Coalition was formed to again take on Napoleon.

Military coalition: an alliance of countries that work together to achieve a common military goal.

Grande Armée: The large French Army under the command of Napoleon. This army had many military successes, not only because of Napoleon's brilliant strategies, but also because the officers were promoted based on merit. This concept was very different from other countries of the time, where officers were typically appointed based on their wealth or family connections. It was said that the mind of Napoleon was worth an extra 40,000 soldiers on the battlefield, and he proved it at the Battle of Austerlitz.

Flank: a way to describe either the far left or far right side of a large group of soldiers.

1. Which French Emperor led France to victory in the Battle of Austerlitz?
2. What was the other name for the Battle of Austerlitz?
3. What is the French phrase describing the very large military under the direction of Napoleon?

Brain Spark:

1. Crusades were intended to reclaim which "holiest" city, which holds special importance to Jews, Christians and Muslims alike?

2. In which ocean did the 2004 tsunami originate?

3. Angkor Wat houses temples dedicated to which two religions?

4. What illness threatens climbers of tall mountains, such as Mount Kilimanjaro, due to low oxygen levels at high altitudes?

Brain Spark

TRAIL OF TEARS

The creation of the United States of America had its heroic moments, but it has had some dark ones as well. One of the darker moments ever undertaken by the U.S. government was its treatment of **Native American** tribes in the 1800s. As America expanded and added new states, the U.S. government wanted to move **Native American** tribes (approximately 60,000 people) out of their locations in the southern states.

In 1830, led by **President Andrew Jackson**, the United States passed the **Indian Removal Act**, which dictated that the Native American tribes must move to <u>reservations</u> in **Oklahoma**, designated as **Indian Territory**. In the first few years, some tribes (Seminole, Chickasaw, Creek, and Choctaw) relocated, but many of the **Cherokee** held out and stayed put. Even the U.S. Supreme Court decided the Cherokee should be able to stay.

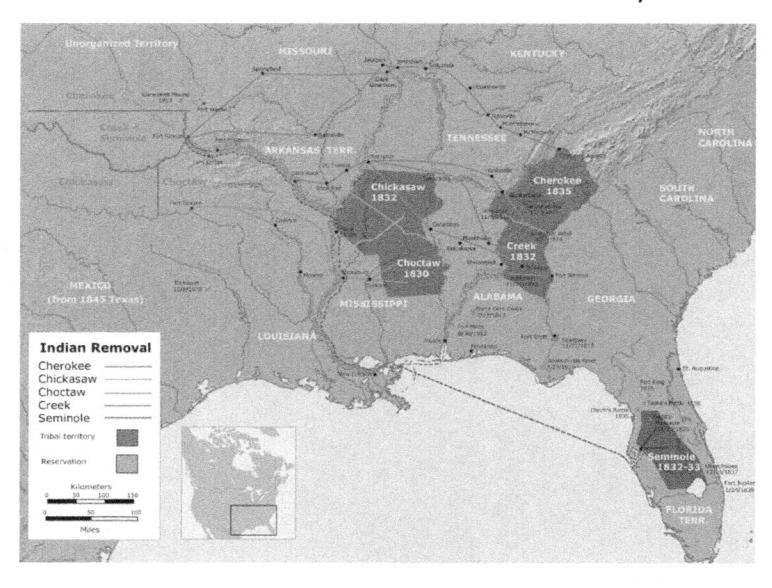

However, President Jackson ignored that ruling. In 1838, Jackson sent in the **U.S. Army** to force their removal at gunpoint. The resulting march to Oklahoma, known as the **Trail of Tears**, spanned 1,000 miles, and thousands of Cherokee died of starvation and sickness on their way to the reservations. Many of the Cherokee also died from cold, as they were used to the warmer weather in Georgia, didn't have shoes or **moccasins**, and weren't dressed for the winter weather.

Reservation: an area of land set aside to be occupied by Native Americans.

Moccasin: a soft leather slipper or shoe. Common type of footwear amongst the different Native American tribes.

1. What was the name of the act that dictated that Native American tribes in the southern U.S. should be moved to Oklahoma?
2. Who was president of the United States when the Indian Removal Act was passed in 1830?
3. What Native American tribe suffered when they were forced to march to Oklahoma in 1838?

Brain Spark:

1. What Napoleonic battle was also known as The Battle of the Three Emperors?
2. What is the name given to the spiritual leader of Tibetan Buddhism?
3. What 1921 act set quotas on how many immigrants could come from certain countries?
4. What future South African president was held in prison on Robben Island for 18 years?

CALIFORNIA GOLD RUSH

In **1848**, a shiny metal was found in the water in **Northern California**; it was gold!

At the time, **California** was not even a state yet. The territory had just recently been taken from **Mexico** after the **Mexican-American War** (1846-1848), and was a very sparsely populated area. In fact, there was no easy way to get from the East Coast of the United States to California without taking serious risks. You could try to travel across the country without marked roads or maps, and hope that you didn't die from animal attacks, disease or getting lost. The safer bet was to take a boat around South America to the Pacific Ocean and on to California, which could take 4-5 months!

When the U.S. public found out about gold lying in the California rivers, there was a mad rush by many to make it to the **West Coast** and find their own piece of gold. The peak of the rush was in **1849**. In fact, the gold rushers were generally known as the **'49ers**. The San Francisco football team is named after those gold rushers.

Initially there was so much gold in the water that you could just **pan** for gold. You would use a pan, scoop up dirt from the side of the river and swirl the dirt around. The gold flakes and little nuggets were heavy enough to stay in the middle of the pan, while the lighter dirt and water would filter out. However, as more and more people were panning, it became harder and harder to find gold just by relying on a pan. Eventually rivers were re-routed so that **riverbeds** could be processed for gold. It is estimated that in the first four years of the 1848 Gold Rush, over 370 tons of gold were recovered (approximately $23 billion in 2021 dollars). The term "**pay dirt**" means making a good profit, and was frequently used back when miners would find a spot rich in gold.

Hundreds of thousands of people moved to California in search of riches, and many ended up staying there. This transformed California from a quiet part of the West Coast into a booming economy, with San Francisco growing from 1,000 to 25,000 people within a year. Interestingly the people who made the most money were those selling the gold digging supplies to the gold rushers. The newfound riches of California had an impact on economies around the world, with farmers in South America, Hawaii, and Australia now able to sell their food to the West Coast. By 1869, a train could transport you from New York to California within days (instead of the 4-5 months it would take by boat).

However, the Gold Rush had **negative** effects too. Many **Native Americans** were pushed off their land, died from attacks or starved because their food sources were ruined by the chemicals used in the mining operations. The mining also had an **environmental** impact, especially when **mercury** was used to help extract gold from the dirt. The **mercury** would just be dumped back into the rivers, which in turn poisoned a lot of waterways. Even today, there are still many lakes and rivers in central California where it is not advisable to eat too much fish because of mercury exposure.

Mercury: a liquid metal that, when ingested or inhaled, can enter the bloodstream and cause damage to the kidneys, lungs, and brain.

1. In what year was gold discovered in California, triggering the California Gold Rush?
2. What three letter tool did gold prospectors use to sift gold out of riverbeds?
3. What liquid metal, used the help extract gold from dirt, poisoned many waterways?

Brain Spark:

1. What U.S. president led the evacuation of Native Americans from their homes in the southern U.S. onto reservations in Oklahoma?
2. What was the name given to the series of battles waged over many decades by Christians against Muslims in an attempt to retake the Holy Land?
3. Which U.S. president oversaw the construction of the Panama Canal?
4. In which year did the legendary massive eruption of Krakatoa take place?

Strange Places and Important Events

THE ABDICATION OF EDWARD VIII

Can you believe that a king would give up his throne in order to get married to the love of his life? It happened in 1936!

King Edward VIII was the King of **England**, and came to the throne in January of 1936 after his father, King George V, passed away. Before becoming king, Prince Edward had fallen in love with the American **socialite Wallis Simpson**, and had started an **affair** with her while she was still married to her second husband.

The British government was quite concerned about this relationship, and there were many unflattering rumors circulating about Mrs. Wallis Simpson.

King Edward VIII

Many objected to the relationship out of fear that Wallis Simpson was only after money and jewelry. Some felt that there was a **constitutional crisis**, since the King of England is the head of the **Anglican Church**, and at the time the Anglican Church forbade the remarriage of divorced people if the ex-spouse was still alive.

When Wallis Simpson divorced her second husband in 1936, King Edward decided that he was going to marry her. The British government made it clear to the King that they wouldn't agree to the marriage. King Edward VIII realized that in order to proceed with marriage, he would have to give up his throne. In December of 1936, he **abdicated** his throne to the great shock of many. His reign as King was one of the shortest in recent English history, lasting less than a year.

Edward's brother became **King George VI**, while Edward was made the **Duke of Windsor**. Wallis Simpson became the Duchess of Windsor.

The **Duke of Windsor** also infamously garnered attention in 1937 when he visited **Adolf Hitler** in Nazi Germany, against the advice of the British government. When World War II broke out, he was eventually moved to the Bahamas where he served as governor.

Wallis Simpson

There continued to be a lot of tension between King George VI, the royal family, and the **Duke of Windsor**, and it was made clear that he was not wanted in Britain. The couple eventually moved to **Paris** (France), where they lived together until his death in 1972.

Socialite: someone who is well-known in social circles. Typically refers to either a wealthy or aristocratic young woman.

Affair: an intimate relationship between two people, when one or both are married to someone else.

Abdicate: to renounce or give up a throne.

1. Who was the father of King Edward VIII?
2. King Edward VIII abdicated the throne of England so that he could marry what woman?
3. What was the name of Edward VIII's brother, who became king after Edward's abdication?

Brain Spark:

1. In 1848, the discovery of gold sparked a "gold rush" in which U.S. State?
2. Which emperor led France to victory in the Battle of Austerlitz?
3. What great dam was constructed in the 1930s, connecting Arizona and Nevada?
4. Which Incan ruler built Machu Picchu?

THE 1917 RUSSIAN EVOLUTION

The early 20th century was a time of great unrest and unhappiness in Russia. In fact, the unrest **culminated** in the 1917 Russian Revolution, which was actually two revolutions as well as a civil war!

The first revolution, also known as the **February Revolution of 1917**, started due to the collapse of the Russian Army during **World War I**. Soldiers were beginning to **mutiny**, and senior military and political leaders were convinced that the unrest in Russia would improve if **Tsar Nicolas II** abdicated from power. The Tsar did give up his throne, and the Russian parliament took over. Poor communities around Russia were unhappy with these developments since they were convinced that Russia was still controlled by wealthy families. So, in response, those communities formed "**soviets**," which were small **grassroot** communities.

The soviets and the ruling parliament were in constant opposition to each other. Eventually, the **Bolshevik** party, under **Vladimir Lenin**, became more and more popular as it promised to sign a peace treaty with **Germany**, give land to the farmers, and end the **famine** that was spreading throughout Russia.

The Bolsheviks organized the **Red Guards**, which were **militias** of peasants, former soldiers, and factory workers.

Shortly after, in **October of 1917**, the second revolution occurred when the Red Guards overthrew the government in **Saint Petersburg** (the capital of Russia at the time).

The **Bolsheviks** were a far-left political organization focused on **socialism**. Once they took over power in 1917, they reformed the Russian Empire into a **socialist union**. They also signed a peace treaty with Germany, as they had promised. The Bolsheviks created the **Cheka**, a secret police, that would punish or execute anyone who was an enemy of the people. This period was called the "**Red Terror**."

Vladimir Lenin giving a speech during the revolution in 1917

Russia was drawn into a civil war between the **Reds** (the **Bolsheviks**) and the **White Army** (all those opposed to the Bolsheviks). The **Russian Civil War** lasted over five years, and came to an end when the **Red Army** defeated the White Army.

The outcome of the revolution and the civil war was the Union of Soviet Socialist Republics (**U.S.S.R.**), and the Bolsheviks renamed themselves the **Communist Party** of the Soviet Union. The leader of the new Soviet Union was now Vladimir Lenin.

Culminated: to reach a high point.

Mutiny: a rebellion by soldiers against their commanding officers.

Grassroot: describing a group or organization run by ordinary people.

Famine: an extreme shortage of food.

Militia: a military force made up of ordinary citizens.

1. In what year did the Russian Revolution take place?
2. Who was the leader of the Bolshevik party during the Russian Revolution?
3. What was the name of the Bolshevik secret police that would punish rivals and enemies?

Brain Spark:

1. Who did King Edward VIII marry after abdicating his throne?
2. Which Native American tribe was forced at gun point to march to Oklahoma along the Trail of Tears?
3. What does the word tsunami mean in Japanese?
4. Cape Horn is at the northern part of a passage around South America named for which explorer?

JIM CROW LAWS

Today, Western societies value social equality. The goal of social equality is to have the law treat all people the same regardless of the color of their skin, but that has not always been the case.

In fact, for many years in the southern United States, a set of laws existed that kept Black people from accessing the same places or opportunities as white people. These were called **Jim Crow laws**. No one is sure how they came to be called by that name, although Jim Crow was a **derogatory** term in the 19th century to describe **African Americans**. From the 1850s to the 1870s, the early **minstrel** shows were a popular form of theater. These typically involved white actors painting their faces black while making fun of the singing and dancing of Black slaves. One of the earliest white minstrel actors had created a song and dance number called "**Jump Jim Crow**."

The **American Civil War** was a bloody battle that saw an end to the terrible slavery that held many Black people in chains in the south for centuries. However, when the slaves were freed in 1863, many southern whites did not see them as equals. As a result, the southern Democrats enacted a number of local and state laws that kept Black people and white people apart, limiting many Black people's rights.

Some of the more common Jim Crow laws allowed for **segregated** schools, restaurants, and buses. Famously, **Rosa Parks** became a major figure in the **Civil Rights** movement when she refused to **adhere** to the Jim Crow law that stated she had to give up her seat to a white passenger in 1955. Jim Crow Laws became officially illegal throughout the country in 1964 when

Rosa Parks gets fingerprinted in 1956

President Lyndon B. Johnson helped pass the **Civil Rights Act**.

Segregated: separated, usually by race.

Adhere: to follow the practices of something.

Derogatory: disrespectful.

1. What was the name of the set of laws in the American south that kept Black people segregated from white people?
2. In 1955, who famously refused to adhere to the Jim Crow law that stated she had to give up her bus seat to a white passenger?
3. Who was President of the United States when the Civil Rights Act was passed in 1964?

Brain Spark:

1. Vladimir Lenin was the leader of which party during the Russian Revolution?
2. The San Francisco 49ers, named after the California gold rush of 1848 and 1849, play which professional sport?
3. Tibet is controlled by which Asian country?
4. Which volcano is the highest mountain in Japan?

ACLU

Although **freedom of speech** is a fundamental **right** in the United States (in fact, the **First Amendment** to the **U.S. Constitution** was passed in 1791 specifically to protect the freedom of speech), it may come as a surprise that freedom of speech was not protected by the Supreme Court of the United States during World War I.

Several people were convicted of anti-war speeches during World War I under the **Espionage Act of 1917**, which made it illegal to protest against the war. These convictions were appealed all the way to the U.S. Supreme Court in 1919, and the Supreme Court decided that anti-war speech was not allowed.

The National Civil Liberties Bureau (**NCLB**) was created by attorneys who disagreed with these decisions, and felt that freedom of speech, especially anti-war speech, should be protected. The NCLB transformed into the **ACLU** (**American Civil Liberties Union**) in the early 1920s to focus more on education and activism.

One of the most famous cases early in the life of the ACLU was the **Scopes Monkey Trial**. A young high school teacher, **John Scopes**, was accused of violating the **Butler Act** (which made it illegal for public schools in Tennessee to teach **human evolution**) in 1925. The ACLU helped stage the trial, and Mr. Scopes purposefully **incriminated** himself, in order to bring attention to this law. Although Mr. Scopes was found guilty (and had to pay a $100 fine), the case was overturned shortly thereafter. The ACLU still considered this a victory since they were able to shine a negative light on the Butler Act.

Over the next hundred years, the ACLU would actively get involved in cases that impacted the freedom of speech and civil rights. The organization would pride itself in supporting the civil rights of those who even had **unpopular** viewpoints, or may even be despised by society. In fact, there was an infamous case in **Skokie, Illinois**. In 1977, an American Nazi wanted to stage a rally in Skokie, a town with a large Jewish population. The town of Skokie refused permission for the rally, and even passed **ordinances** to prevent him from holding a rally. The ACLU came to his defense, and eventually won the right for him to be able to exercise his freedom of speech (no matter how **abhorrent** that speech may be). This was deeply unpopular, and many ACLU members left the ACLU because of it.

The ACLU and its members have been perceived as liberal and progressive by many within American society. In fact, over the last few decades, some would argue that the ACLU has become more and more politically involved compared to its early roots of primarily defending civil liberties in court.

The ACLU has grown into a large organization, with offices in all 50 U.S. states, and over 100 attorneys who work with thousands of volunteer attorneys. No other organization has appeared more often before the Supreme Court to argue their cases than the ACLU.

Abhorrent: deserving of disgust and strong dislike; loathsome.

Human evolution: the process by which modern humans developed, over the course of many thousands of years, from ape-like ancestors. This stands in contrast to "creationism", which is the religious idea that humans were created in their current form by a god.

Incriminated: to make a person appear guilty of wrongdoing or a crime.

Ordinance: a type of law passed by a local authority (i.e.: a town or county).

1. Which (numbered) amendment to the U.S. Constitution guarantees the freedom of speech?
2. Which 1917 act made it illegal to protest against World War I?
3. The ACLU helped defend a teacher accused of teaching human evolution to students in Tennessee. What was the name of that teacher?

Brain Spark:
1. What was the name of the shows, common in the south, wherein white actors sang and danced with their faces painted black?
2. After abdicating his throne, Edward VIII became Duke of what?
3. Which sultan led the Muslims against the Christians during the Third Crusade?
4. Although called a "sea", what is the deepest salt-water lake in the world?

AUSCHWITZ

Beyond the general horrors of war, the **genocide** against the Jewish people by the Nazis during World War II is considered one of the worst war crimes in history. Probably no place is more **emblematic** of the **Holocaust** then the concentration and extermination camps at Auschwitz.

After **Germany** invaded **Poland** in 1939, Germany turned **Auschwitz** (a small town southwest of **Krakow** in Poland) from an army barracks into a prisoner of war camp. For the first two years of the war, Polish political prisoners were kept in the camp. However, it wasn't long before the German guards started to torture and execute those prisoners. From 1942 to 1944, freight trains from all over Europe would bring **Jews** (including women and children) to Auschwitz for either **hard labor** or execution.

Children survivors shortly after Auschwitz was liberated

Most of the prisoners and Jews were brought by train, and they would walk through a large gate with the inscription "***Arbeit Macht Frei***" (German for "work sets you free"). They would then be processed and inspected by Nazi doctors and officers. Men who were felt to be in shape to do hard labor were sent in one direction. They would have their heads shaved, and their arms tattooed with a serial number to track them. **Jews** would wear **yellow stars** on their prison gear. Women, children, the elderly, and frail men were typically told that they were going to be taking a shower, and moved into large gas chambers (that could fit over 800 people at a time). **Zyklon B** was the primary poison used by the Nazis. It was a type of cyanide poison, which would stop the cells in the body from working. All the prisoners were dead within 20 minutes of being locked in the chambers. Their bodies would then be removed and brought to large **crematoriums** to be cremated. But first, their glasses, jewelry, and any gold teeth were removed so that the Germans could melt those down for money.

Some of the women and children however were kept for medical experiments by the infamous **Dr. Josef Mengele**, known as **"The Angel of Death."** If they survived the experiments, most were killed and dissected for further research.

The prisoners at Auschwitz were kept in terrible conditions, with limited food and poor hygiene. They were forced to work over 11 hours a day, typically by being outsourced to various factories or jobs around the concentration camp.

One of the largest "employers" of slave labor from the Auschwitz camp was **IG Farben**. IG Farben, a chemical manufacturer, was at the time the largest corporation in Europe (and fourth largest in the world). In a sick twist of fate, IG Farben actually supplied **Zyklon B** to the concentration camps.

In 1942, the German Nazis established the **Final Solution** plan: to kill as many Jews as possible. The Holocaust led to the death of 90% of Polish Jews, and over 65% of the Jewish population in Europe. More than 1.1 million people were murdered at Auschwitz. Overall, 6 million Jews were murdered throughout Europe, and this included about 1 million Jewish children. Jews were not the only ones targeted by the Nazis, although they were the most impacted. The Nazis also went after homosexuals, **Jehovah's Witnesses**, political opponents, and **gypsies**, as well as Germans with mental and physical disabilities.

Hard Labor: heavy manual labor. It is a form of punishment that is forced (meaning there are no other options), and no payment is made for the work performed.

Jehovah's Witness: a type of Christian faith that rejects the trinity of God (in other words, they don't believe that the Father, the Son (Jesus) and the Holy Spirit are one God). They do not celebrate birthdays or Christian religious days, but will memorialize Jesus's death around Easter time. They are conscientious objectors to military service, and will also refuse blood transfusions (even if that transfusion could save their life).

Gypsy: preferably referred to as Roma or Romani, this is an ethnic group of people that originated in India, but migrated to Europe by the 12th century. They are nomads, typically traveling by horse carriage and caravans around Europe. They were persecuted, and many were enslaved in Medieval Europe. There still is persecution of the Roma around the world.

Genocide: the deliberate murder of a large number of people from a specific country or ethnic group.

Holocaust: destruction on a large scale. The Holocaust was the genocide of European Jews during World War II.

Emblematic: symbolic.

1. In which country was the Auschwitz concentration camp located?
2. What infamous Nazi doctor was known as "The Angel of Death"?
3. Which German chemical manufacturer manufactured Zyklon B, a poison used in the execution of millions of Jews?

Brain Spark:

1. Which 1917 act allowed for protestors of World War I to be arrested in the United States?
2. In which year did the Russian Revolution take place?
3. Which French king was executed during the French Revolution?
4. Angkor Wat was originally dedicated to which Hindu god?

NATO

To fight the Nazi and Japanese empires during World War II, the Allies (primarily the United States and **Great Britain**) had to work with the **Soviet Union** and their leader, Joseph Stalin. After Nazi Germany was defeated, the leaders of the U.S., Great Britain, and the Soviet Union (U.S.S.R.) met in **Potsdam** (a small town outside of **Berlin,** Germany) to plan how to split up control of Germany and organize the new post-war world order.

It didn't take long for the relationship between the West and the U.S.S.R. to deteriorate. World War II came to an end when Japan surrendered in August of 1945. Already by 1946, there were concerns that the U.S.S.R. was supporting communist activity in **Greece** and also creating military pressure on **Turkey** to give up control of the **Bosphorus Strait**. The response by the West (which at this time included the U.S., Great Britain, and France) was to formalize agreements to protect themselves from another world war. By 1947, U.S. President Truman established the **Truman Doctrine** with the intention of blocking the expansion of Soviet and communist influence.

Because of these concerns, **NATO** was formed in 1949. The **North Atlantic Treaty Organization** (NATO) is an agreement amongst member countries that they would come to each other's defense if any country were to ever attack them (specifically stated in **Article 5** of the treaty). Article 5 has only been triggered once, and that was after the attack on the U.S. on September 11, 2001.

While it started out as 12 member countries, NATO now has 30 members (the U.S., Canada and 28 countries in Europe). When Germany joined NATO in 1955, the U.S.S.R. responded by creating the **Warsaw Pact**. Similar to NATO, it was a defensive pact between the Soviet Union and the Eastern European countries whose communist governments were loyal to Russia (**Poland, Czechoslovakia, Hungary, East Germany, Bulgaria, Romania,** and **Albania**).

Brain Spark

Even when the **Cold War** came to an end in 1991 with the collapse of the Soviet Union, **NATO** decided to continue as a defensive alliance. It continued to add members in Central and Eastern Europe, right up to the border of Russia.

NATO Enlargement
- 1949 Belgium, Canada, Denmark, France, Iceland, Italy, Luxembourg, the Netherlands, Norway, Portugal, U.K., U.S.
- 1952 Greece and Turkey
- 1955 West Germany (East and West Germany were unified in 1990)
- 1982 Spain
- 1999 Czech Republic, Hungary, and Poland
- 2004 Bulgaria, Estonia, Latvia, Lithuania, Romania, Slovakia, and Slovenia
- 2009 Albania and Croatia
- 2017 Montenegro
- 2019 North Macedonia ★ (Pending ratification by member states)

Russia has not been happy about this expansion of NATO, as it sees it as a threat to its own security. It is one of the reasons that Russia used as an excuse to invade **Ukraine** in February 2022.

NATO did not have to fight actively during the entire Cold War. However, after 1991, it intervened in the Bosnian War and the Kosovo War (two wars that occurred after **Yugoslavia** collapsed in 1992). In 2001, after the 9/11 attacks in the U.S., NATO also participated in the War in Afghanistan.

Bosphorus Strait: an important natural waterway in northwest Turkey which forms part of the border between Asia and Europe.

1. What was the name of the Cold War era doctrine created by a U.S. President with the intention of blocking the expansion of communist influence?
2. What does the acronym NATO stand for?
3. What "pact" was the Soviet response to NATO?

Brain Spark:

1. Can you name a Nazi concentration camp that had "Arbeit Macht Frei" inscribed on a large gate at the entrance?

2. What was the name given to the set of laws designed to separate Black and white people in the southern United States?

3. The Trail of Tears led Native Americans on a march to which U.S. territory (that is now a state)?

4. What is the name of the mental disorder wherein people abnormally interpret their emotions and the world, leading to troubled thoughts, delusions, disorganization, and difficulty in maintaining relationships due to a withdrawal from reality?

Brain Spark

THE KOREAN WAR

Would you believe that one of the most destructive wars after World War II was a war that ended in 1953, with a peace treaty that was never signed? It was the **Korean War**, and this would explain a lot of today's ongoing tension on the Korean **peninsula**.

Korea has had a troubled history over the last two centuries. Although it was officially occupied by **Imperial Japan** in 1910, the Japanese had already been exerting control over Korea starting in the late 1800s.

When the Japanese surrendered in August 1945, the **Soviet Union** and the **United States** decided to split Korea into two pieces along the **38th parallel**, forming North and South Korea. The Soviets controlled North Korea and helped install a **socialist** government under the dictatorship of **Kim Il-Sung**. A **capitalist** government was set up by the Americans in South Korea.

The South Korean government was weak, and had been struggling with communist insurgents in South Korea. The North Korean leadership felt that this had weakened South Korea, and that the South Koreans would welcome an invasion by the North Korean army.

Kim Il-Sung received permission from Soviet leader **Joseph Stalin** and China's leader **Mao Zedong** to attack South Korea. The Soviets supplied military equipment and the Chinese provided further manpower. When the North Koreans attacked in June 1950, the **United Nations** (U.N.) responded by organizing a military response under the leadership of the United States.

At the time, the United States was focusing its military strategy on supporting Western Europe, organizing their nuclear forces and winding down the immense military machine that had helped win World War II. In fact, the U.S. military size was brought down over **90%** from over 12 million soldiers to 1.5 million! They had to release soldiers back into the regular work force, and they would end up selling or melting down much of the military equipment.

The United States was not prepared for this war. So, it wasn't a surprise that the North Koreans were able to successfully push the poorly equipped South Koreans and U.S. soldiers all the way to the southern tip of South Korea.

The U.S. government under **President Harry S. Truman** dedicated significant financial support to rebuild the U.S. military. Under the leadership **of General Douglas MacArthur**, the South Koreans and U.N. forces (which were primarily U.S. soldiers) were able to push the North Koreans back to the 38th parallel line. In fact, General MacArthur was able to push his forces North of the parallel line, despite warnings from President Truman that this could **enrage** the Chinese.

As the U.S. was making progress towards the Chinese border, the Chinese decided by December 1950 to officially participate in the war in support of North Korea (although unofficially they had been participating since the start of the conflict). This turned the tide of war against the U.N. forces in the south.

Tension and frustration grew between President Truman and General MacArthur. MacArthur wrongly believed that by crossing the 38th parallel the Chinese would not get involved, and he also felt that he should be able to use nuclear weapons against the Chinese, if needed. General MacArthur was relieved of duty by President Truman.

Eventually a stalemate developed along the 38th parallel between the North and South Koreans. This stalemate dragged out over the next three years with many casualties as both forces continued to attack and bombard each other with **artillery**. Finally, in July 1953, the two sides signed an **armistice**, agreeing to return to the 38th parallel as the boundary between the two countries.

To this day, there has been no peace treaty between these two warring nations. In fact, as recently as 2013, the North Koreans claimed that the armistice was invalid and that they were again in a state of war with South Korea. The United States lost about 40,000 soldiers during the Korean War, with another 100,000 wounded. The civilian populations of both North and South Korea suffered the most, with close to three million civilians dying during the war.

The 38th parallel is widely known as the "**DMZ**" (**demilitarized zone**). It is 160 miles long, and 2.5 miles wide. Despite the name, it is actually the most heavily guarded area in the world, and is often referred to as "**no-man's land.**" There have been many incursions across this zone, primarily by the North Koreans who had built tunnels in order to quickly infiltrate South Korea.

Peninsula: a large piece of land that extends from the mainland, and is surrounded by water on three sides.

Artillery: heavy guns that can launch a very large projectile a long distance. These are typically pulled by trucks or are even positioned on top of large trucks.

Enrage: to trigger an anger in someone.

Armistice: an agreement between warring nations to stop fighting with the hope of negotiating a lasting peace.

1. Who was the leader of the communist North Korean government at the start of the Korean War?

2. What numbered line marks the contested boundary between North and South Korea?

3. Despite being so heavily guarded, what is the 38th parallel also commonly known as?

Brain Spark:

1. What "pact" was the Soviet response to NATO?

2. The ACLU supported the right of Nazis to march in what Illinois town in 1977?

3. What phrase meaning "making a good profit" arose from miners who found gold-rich soil in the 1800s?

4. Which country's failed investment in a trade route through Panama led to it joining the United Kingdom?

Brain Spark

CUBAN MISSILE CRISIS

Many people alive in the 1960s never fully realized just how close the world came to a catastrophic war unmatched in destruction. In October **1962**, the **Cuban Missile Crisis** brought the **United States** and the **Soviet Union** to the brink of **nuclear war**.

After the U.S. had positioned nuclear-tipped missiles in Turkey near the Soviet border, and shortly after a failed invasion of **Cuba** in 1961 (the "**Bay of Pigs Invasion**"), Cuba struck a secret deal with the Soviet Union to position Soviet nuclear missiles on the island. **Fidel Castro**, who was the Cuban leader, was hoping that these missiles would discourage any further American invasion plans on Cuban soil.

When U.S. President **John F Kennedy** found **out** about the secret buildup thanks to **U2 spy plane** photos, he ordered a naval <u>blockade</u> of Cuba. He didn't want any more missiles deployed to an island that is only 100 miles away from the U.S.

The Soviet Union was very upset by this, and this triggered tension between the U.S. and the Soviet Union. The Soviet Union was not going to allow the U.S. to stop their ships from heading to Cuba, nor allow their ships to be boarded and searched. President Kennedy prepared the U.S. military for nuclear readiness, with bombers on 15-minute stand-by to take off, and also ready to invade Cuba.

At the last minute, and after secret negotiations between President Kennedy and Soviet leader **Nikita Khrushchev**, an agreement was made to remove the missiles from Cuba, as long as the U.S. would remove its missiles from **Turkey**. The U.S. also promised not to invade Cuba. Many historians believe that this is the closest we have ever come to a full nuclear war.

were known as the **Khmer Rouge** (a name given to them by the French, since **rouge** means **red** in French and is typically associated with communism).

Pol Pot and the communist government launched **radical** reforms. All men and women had to wear the same black uniform. Money was abolished, banks (and banking records) were destroyed, so that everyone could truly be "**equal.**" The goal was to create an **agrarian** society that would be totally self-sufficient. To this end, city people were "evacuated" from the cities and moved into the countryside in order to work on farms. Anyone who was of a different ethnicity or different religion (Christian or Muslim), or was seen as a threat to the communist regime, was sent to "re-education" camps where they were **executed**.

Once the cities were evacuated, factories fell into disrepair as they were empty. Hospitals were closed. Schools were closed, and the teachers were eyed with suspicion (and many were executed as well). It was a complete disaster. The city people didn't know how to farm, and the country had run out of money to buy appropriate farming equipment, fertilizer and pesticides. A **famine** was triggered. The government dealt with this by **executing** those responsible for the farming failures. It was just a matter of time before the government started executing anyone within the government who would disagree with Pol Pot's leadership.

China was the only country providing support to Pol Pot's regime, in the form of advisors, as well as financial and food aid. In fact, Pol Pot interacted frequently with **Mao Zedong** (the Chinese leader) and **Kim Il-Sung** (North Korean leader), and often had their public support.

The Khmer Rouge, and Pol Pot in particular, were worried that Vietnam would invade Cambodia. Therefore, the Khmer Rouge pursued a pre-emptive attack against Vietnam in early 1978, which led to months of border **skirmishes**. By December 1978, Vietnam responded with a coordinated counterattack and was able to take control of **Phnom Penh** (the capital city of Cambodia).

For the next ten years, Pol Pot would alternatively hide in **Thailand** or the mountains of Cambodia, and organize ongoing resistance to the **Vietnamese** control of Cambodia.

With the **Berlin Wall** coming down in 1989, followed by the collapse of the Soviet Union in 1991, there was a growing call for peace and democracy in Cambodia. However, this did not stop Pol Pot from orchestrating continued resistance, with the Khmer Rouge still controlling some mountain territories. The Khmer Rouge continued to disintegrate as more and more senior leaders left Pol Pot, and as more farmers felt taken advantage of by Pol Pot's policies.

Eventually, Pol Pot was arrested in 1997 and imprisoned. He died shortly thereafter from heart failure.

It is estimated that close to three million people, approximately 25% of the Cambodian population, were murdered during what is now known as the **Cambodian Genocide**.

Atrocity: a very cruel act of violence.

Carpet bombing: a strategy that relies on covering an area with bombs without choosing a specific target. It has legally been considered a war crime to carpet bomb civilian areas since 1977.

Radical: an extreme type of change.

Agrarian: relating to farming and cultivating fields.

Famine: extreme lack of food.

Skirmish: an irregular attack between small military groups usually along a border.

1. Pol Pot was the dictator of what Southeast Asian country?
2. What was the name given to the communist revolutionaries who were led by Pol Pot?
3. What is the capital city of Cambodia?

Brain Spark:

1. Who was the U.S. President during the Cuban Missile Crisis?
2. What is the name of the coalition of North American and European nations created in 1949, designed to guarantee military support for each other in the event of an invasion?
3. Who was the tsar of Russia leading into the Russian Revolution?
4. What is the word for a large and powerful earthquake that occurs at a subduction zone and commonly seen in the Pacific and Indian Ocean?

THE SPACE RACE

Can you believe that astronauts walked on the moon over fifty years ago?! Would you believe that the computers on their spaceship were as powerful as your pocket calculator? How could a country in the 1960s get to the moon when its technology was so far inferior to anything we can even think of now?

As you may remember, the United States and the Soviet Union were locked in a "**cold war**" that started shortly after World War II. Both countries were trying to outdo each other in terms of **ballistic** missiles that could deliver nuclear weapons at high speeds from very long distances. It wasn't a surprise that these two countries considered space the next area to compete in, and then dominate. What did come as a surprise was when the Soviet Union launched the first **satellite**, "Sputnik", in 1957. This triggered the "**Sputnik Crisis**" in the United States; it showed that the entire North American continent was vulnerable to Soviet missile technology.

The United States government responded by drastically increasing their spending on military defense, their investment in education (with the hope of getting more American researchers), and the creation of **NASA** (the **National Aeronautics and Space Administration**) in 1958.

The United States fell even more behind when the Soviets launched the first person into space, **Yuri Gagarin**, in 1961. President **John F. Kennedy** gave a speech to congress a month later, announcing that the U.S. had plans to put a man on the moon by the end of the 1960s. This plan became known as the **Apollo program**.

Ultimately, the United States had 400,000 people working on the Apollo program, and the support of 20,000 universities and companies! In July of 1969, the United States made it to the moon. The Apollo 11 mission landed two American astronauts (**Neil Armstrong** and **Buzz Aldrin**) on the **Sea of Tranquility** (an area of the moon that NASA felt would be a safe landing zone).

The Soviets struggled with their manned lunar landing program, suffering several setbacks as their large rockets would explode on the launch pads. In 1974, the Soviets gave up on their attempts to put a **cosmonaut** on the moon. However, they didn't give up on space, and were able to launch several space stations.

U.S. President **Richard Nixon** and Soviet Premier **Leonid Brezhnev** worked on developing a **détente** (an easing of relations between the two competing superpowers). In 1975, an Apollo spaceship was able to **rendez-vous** with a Soviet **Soyuz** spaceship, where U.S. astronauts and Soviet cosmonauts worked together in space.

This period of calm between the two space superpowers was short lived, and it wasn't until after the collapse of the Soviet Union in 1991 that the two countries started to work together in space again. Initially, this involved the U.S. **space shuttle** visiting the Russian space station **Mir**, followed by both countries working together to build the **International Space Station.**

The **Space Race** had a significant impact on the world, accelerating new technologies, including solar panels, water filtration systems, better firefighting equipment, air purifiers, shock absorbers and computers.

Some historians believe that the Soviets spent so much money and effort on their space programs that it helped weaken their economy, which in turn accelerated the end to the Soviet Union.

Ballistic missile: a powerful missile that requires significant energy and fuel to get into space, but then falls back to earth by the force of gravity.

Artificial satellite: an object purposefully put into orbit around the earth (although humans have also put artificial satellites around most planets in our solar system).

Cosmonaut: a Soviet or Russian astronaut.

Rendez-vous: a French word describing a meeting that occurs at a predetermined location and time.

1. What was the name of the first Soviet satellite in space?
2. Who was the first person to go to space?
3. What is the term for a Soviet or Russian astronaut?

Brain Spark:

1. What was the name of the dictator who took control of Cambodia in 1975?
2. Which corn cob pipe-smoking General commanded the U.S. forces during the Korean War before being removed from his command by President Truman?
3. Who was President of the United States when the Civil Rights Act was passed in 1964?
4. What is the name of the Buddhist and Hindu beliefs that, after death, a soul is reborn into a new body?

Strange Places and Important Events

PENTAGON PAPERS

What would you do if you had access to <u>**classified**</u> files that proved the government was lying? Would you make them public? Would that be wrong, or right? These were the questions surrounding the release of the **Pentagon Papers**.

The **Vietnam War** was the most controversial U.S. war of the 20th century. It was a war without being an official war; the United States never actually declared a war. Instead, U.S. presidents considered their actions to be a **police action** in **Vietnam**, as they were only sending in "**military advisors**."

After World War II, the United States, and the western powers (France and England) were very concerned about the spread of **communism**, and in Asia they were worried about the growing influence of **China**. Shortly after World War II, a war broke out in **Indochina (Vietnam, Laos,** and **Cambodia)** between France and Southern Vietnam on one side, and the Northern Vietnamese forces under the leadership of **Ho Chi Minh** (a communist revolutionary supported by the Chinese). This war lasted nine years. In 1954, after the French suffered a significant military defeat at **Dien Bien Phu**, they came to an agreement to split Vietnam in to two parts: North Vietnam and South Vietnam.

The United States was supporting the French during that first **Indochina** war, and were not happy that the French had left the war. The United States continued to support the South Vietnamese military with money, equipment and by sending "**military advisors**" to help train the South Vietnamese army. This was the beginning of the unofficial **Vietnam War**. It quickly became an unpopular war in the U.S., as up to 3 million Americans were sent to Vietnam to fight for a cause they didn't quite understand.

In 1967, the Secretary of Defense **Robert McNamara** had high level military officers and historians write a top-secret report and history of the Vietnam War. **Daniel Ellsberg**, who had worked on the report and was opposed to the war, made photocopies of over 3,000 pages of the report. In 1971, he handed those copies over to the **New York Times**, which published segments of the report. The decision by a large newspaper to print top secret information was very controversial, and the U.S. government was very upset. The government tried to stop the newspaper from printing more. Another famous newspaper, the **Washington Post**, started printing articles about the **Pentagon Papers** as well! The U.S. government again sued to get them to stop. The battle over the publishing of the reports went all the way to the **Supreme Court**, which decided that the papers could be published.

The **Pentagon Papers** revealed strategies and activities that were quite shocking because they were sometimes the opposite of what four **consecutive** U.S. presidents (Truman, Eisenhower, Kennedy and Johnson) had told the American people or told the U.S. congress.

It became clear that the fighting in Vietnam was primarily to stop China from expanding its influence in Asia. It showed that the U.S. had interfered with the South Vietnamese government, even possibly facilitating the **assassination** of the South Vietnamese president (he was replaced by generals that were far more friendly to the United States). The Pentagon papers also revealed that although American soldiers were only sent to train the South Vietnamese, it was the intention of the U.S. President to have those soldiers actively fight the North Vietnamese.

This report infuriated the American public, and had a very negative impact on the credibility of the U.S. government.

Classified: secret information that can not be released to the public.

Consecutive: following one after the other; in a row.

1. Government secrets of which "war" were spilled with the release of the Pentagon Papers?
2. What was the name of the man who copied the Pentagon Papers?
3. Which newspaper first published the Pentagon Papers?

Brain Spark:
1. What was the name of the American space program designed to put a man on the moon? (Hint: the 11th launch of the program succeeded in 1969.)
2. Who was the Soviet leader during the Cuban Missile Crisis?
3. Formerly known as the NCLB, what group was created to defend civil rights in the United States, especially the freedom of speech?
4. Which pope launched the First Crusade?

Brain Spark

STONEWALL RIOTS

Homosexuality has been a controversial social topic for thousands of years. In some societies and cultures, it has been tolerated, or even accepted; in others, it has been considered criminal.

Up until the early 1970s in the United States, homosexuality was considered a mental disorder, and often treated as a crime. For many years, members of the LGBT community (lesbian, gay, bisexual and transgender) could only socialize in secret establishments.

There were some neighborhoods in the U.S. that had high concentrations of gay and lesbian inhabitants. Some of the more famous locations were **San Francisco** in California, and **Greenwich Village** in New York City.

Many of the bars and nightclubs **frequented** by gays and lesbians at the time were run by **organized crime** (the **Mafia**). They would provide cheap alcohol, areas to mingle and dance, and often pay-off the police departments to minimize the risk of police raids.

The most famous gay nightclub in **New York City** in the 1960s was the **Stonewall Inn** (on **Christopher Street**). Typically, in those years, during a raid, club-goers would show their identification cards. Some would get arrested, and often the alcohol would be confiscated by the police department. On the last weekend in June of 1969, several undercover police officers went into the Stonewall Inn to initiate a raid. However, this raid turned into a violent confrontation that spilled into the streets. The riots grew larger as patrons from other local bars, as well as other neighbors, joined in.

Although the police were able to bring some calm to the streets by the next morning, new riots broke out the following night. Many in the gay and lesbian community wanted to see a change; they wanted to be accepted by the larger community and no longer have to rely on mafia-run clubs and police pay-offs.

Strange Places and Important Events

This didn't stop police raids though, as more raids were ordered around New York City over the next few years. This in turn triggered an increase in "**gay activism.**" On the one-year anniversary of the **Stonewall Riots**, the first **Gay Pride** marches took place in New York, Los Angeles, and Chicago. This was the beginning of a change in perception of homosexuals in the United States, with a growing focus on their civil rights. In 1973, the **American Psychiatric Association** decided that homosexuality was no longer considered a mental disorder.

Organized crime: criminal behavior that is controlled by large groups.

Frequent: (when used as a verb) to go to or attend regularly.

1. What was the name of the nightclub, popular with homosexuals, that was raided, sparking a massive riot between club goers and police?
2. In what city was the Stonewall Inn located?
3. In what year did the Stonewall Riots occur?

Brain Spark:

1. What was the name of the confidential report released to the New York Times in 1971 outlining lies and failures associated with the Vietnam War?
2. What was the name for the Cambodian communist revolutionaries led by Pol Pot?
3. What Nazi doctor was known as "The Angel of Death"?
4. What was the French term for the very large army under the command of Napoleon?

Brain Spark

KENT STATE SHOOTINGS

Who would have thought that, in the 20th century, U.S. soldiers would open fire on U.S. university students? On May 4th, 1970, that is exactly what happened.

The 1960s saw an escalation of protests against the **Vietnam War**. Many of those protests happened on **university** and **college** campuses around the United States. As the Vietnam War dragged on, the American public was more and more frustrated with the course of the war.

On April 30, 1970, U.S. President **Nixon** announced an attack on **Cambodia** as part of his strategy to undermine the **North Vietnamese** army. The North Vietnamese had been relying on unpopulated sections of eastern Cambodia (a neighboring country to the west of Vietnam) as areas to withdraw and resupply their troops. Schools around the United States saw significant protests on their campuses the next day.

Kent State University is a public university in **Kent, Ohio**. On May 1st, 1970, students started to gather in the center of the campus to protest the war. Unfortunately, these protests progressed into riots and vandalism around the campus and in the local town. Due to the violence, local town officials contacted the governor of Ohio, requesting assistance. The Ohio **National Guard** was sent in on May 2nd, and by the time they arrived on the campus they found that the **ROTC** building on campus was burning.

Between May 2nd and May 4th, there were ongoing protests and confrontations between student protestors and the National Guardsmen. It eventually led to the National Guard getting pelted with stones. The soldiers initially relied on firing **tear gas** canisters, but those were not successful in **dispersing** the crowd.

The soldiers continued to try to control the crowd without success. At about noon, 29 of the 77 soldiers fired their weapons. Four students were killed and nine were injured. The soldiers claimed that they feared for their lives, although the closest victim was over 70 feet away.

This tragedy, as well as the **Jackson State killings** that occurred just two weeks later when police officers fired on students at Jackson State in Mississippi, prompted two different reactions around the country. Students became more and more convinced of the importance to end the war. The Nixon administration convened the **President's Commission on Campus Unrest**, to study growing unrest and violence on college campuses around the country. The commission found that the Kent State shootings were **unjustified**, and that soldiers should not bring loaded rifles to confront student demonstrators.

University vs college: In the U.S., colleges typically are smaller schools for undergraduate work (bachelor's degree). A university tends to be bigger, with more types of bachelor's degrees offered, as well as post-graduate degrees (such as masters and doctorate degrees).

National Guard: every U.S. state has a National Guard, which acts as a military force serving as a back-up reserve for the U.S. Army and U.S. Air Force. Most National Guard soldiers serve part-time, and have full-time non-military jobs. They can be called to participate in a war if called upon by the U.S. government. Otherwise, they are available to each state's governor for natural or man-made disasters.

ROTC: stands for Reserve Officer Training Corps. These are training programs at colleges and universities around the U.S. that prepare students to become officers in one of the military branches (Navy, Air Force, Marines or Army). The ROTC students receive scholarships that cover all or part of their tuition, and a monthly stipend.

Tear gas: also known as "mace." It is a chemical weapon that triggers the tear glands. It also causes eye pain and difficulty breathing. While it is commonly used by police forces around the world to help control violent crowds, it is actually illegal to use it during a war, as decided by the Geneva Convention of 1925.

Disperse: to spread over a wide area.

1. Who was President of the United States when the Kent State Shootings occurred?
2. The demonstrations at Kent State that resulted in student deaths were in response to the U.S. invasion of which country?
3. In which state is Kent State University located?

Brain Spark:

1. Riots arising from a raid at which New York City nightclub became a steppingstone for gay rights activism?
2. What was the name of the location on the moon where Buzz Aldrin and Neil Armstrong landed in 1969?
3. The Truman Doctrine was designed to stop what political and economic philosophy from spreading?
4. What was the name of the act passed by the U.S. government in 1830 that forced the movement of Native American tribes to reservations in Oklahoma?

IRAN CONTRA AFFAIR

Scandals are nothing new when it comes to politics. Many U.S. presidents have been embroiled in controversy, even the popular ones! President Ronald Reagan was no different. During Reagan's second term, the **Iran Contra scandal,** and his role in it, occupied much of the nation's attention.

In late 1979, when 52 Americans were taken hostage in **Tehran** (the capital city of **Iran**), U.S. President Jimmy Carter **retaliated** by banning all weapon sales to Iran.

This sanction became a problem for Iran during the 1980s, since all of their military equipment was American-made at the time, and they were in the middle of a war against **Iraq**. Senior officials in the Reagan administration were worried that Iran (although clearly an enemy of the U.S.) would start buying weapons from the Soviet Union, and possibly become more friendly with the Soviet Union (the archenemy of the U.S. at the time).

These senior officials came up with a plan where they would secretly sell weapons to Iran using middlemen, and even used the weapons as **leverage** to help free hostages from **Lebanon**. This was a problem, since at the time it was an official policy of the U.S. not to negotiate with terrorists or hostage takers.

At the same time, on the other side of the world, there was a socialist government in **Nicaragua** (a small country in **Central America**) struggling with a rebel military group called the **Contras**. The Contras were actively trying to overthrow the Nicaraguan government. The U.S. supported the Contras' goals since they did not want more **socialism** in Central America. In fact, the CIA had already begun to help the Contras without letting Congress know beforehand. The U.S. Congress passed several laws to stop the government from supporting the Contras, as they didn't want to further interfere in Central American politics. However, the Reagan administration came up with creative (and maybe illegal) ways to try to work around congress's rules to continue sending money and arms to the Contras.

Eventually, these secrets were leaked out to the public, and this became a big **scandal** for Ronald Reagan. Many people were upset that his administration had continued to sell weapons to Iran, and had provided weapons and money to the Contras despite Congress's specific laws.

Congress pursued investigations, and over 30 high level government officials (from the military and the CIA) were **indicted**. U.S. Marine Lieutenant Colonel **Oliver North** became the face of the televised congressional investigation, and admitted that he had misled congress.

Oliver North testifying to congress

Ronald Reagan's vice president at the time was **George H.W. Bush**, who went on to become president from 1989 to 1993. President Bush would end up **pardoning** five of the charged officials, and **pre-emptively** pardoned former Defense Secretary **Caspar Weinberger** before he went to trial.

Retaliate: to hurt someone in return for having been hurt yourself.

Leverage: power.

Scandal: an event or act regarded as wrong and looked upon badly by the public.

Indicted: to formally accuse someone with a serious crime.

Pardon: to officially release someone from punishment.

Pre-emptive: taking an action in order to prevent something else from happening.

1. Who was President of the United States during the Iran-Contra Affair?
2. What country were the rebel Contras from?
3. Which Marine Lieutenant Colonel became the face of the televised Iran-Contra investigation?

Brain Spark:
1. At what Ohio university did U.S. National Guardsmen open fire on protesting students in 1970?
2. What Secretary of Defense ordered a top-secret report on Vietnam, later known as the Pentagon Papers?
3. Named for a line of latitude on a map, what numbered "parallel" line marks a demilitarized border separating North and South Korea?
4. The United States acquired California in early 1848 from which country?

Brain Spark

CHERNOBYL

Nuclear power is a clean and effective source of energy, and incredibly powerful. You might have heard of nuclear bombs, which utilize this energy source for destruction. In fact, this energy source can provide a greater good by providing the power for electricity.

Uranium (a radioactive element) creates heat as it falls apart through **nuclear fission** (a process where atoms split apart and release energy). This heat is used to boil water and create steam, and in turn the steam moves turbines to generate electricity.

The main problem with nuclear energy is that it creates **nuclear waste**, which is the by-product of creating this energy. Nuclear waste gives off **radiation**, which is a type of energy that can be quite harmful, since it can penetrate the cells of all living organisms. Radiation exposure can lead to burns, illness and even cancer. If the radiation is powerful enough, it can kill people pretty quickly.

Luckily, nuclear power plants are quite good at controlling these issues and disposing of these wasteful products safely. At the start of 2022, there were 55 nuclear power plants in 28 U.S. states. Most Americans live within 50 miles of a nuclear reactor! But what if all of the safety measures fail?

In 1986, when Russia was still known as the **Soviet Union,** there was a catastrophic failure at the **Chernobyl** nuclear power plant. Chernobyl was near the town of Pripyat, **Ukraine**, about 60 miles from **Kyiv**, the capital of Ukraine. Due to a flawed design and poorly trained workers, there was an explosion in Reactor #4, followed by a fire. The release of radiation from the explosion affected over 7,000 square miles of Europe, and the radiation effects impacted the health of people for decades. Radiation can still be detected near the Chernobyl site today.

What's worse, the Soviet Union compounded the issue. At the time, their government was in a rivalry with the United States (known as the **Cold War**), and attempted to cover up their disaster to avoid embarrassment, likely costing more lives. While the official death toll was 31, many scientific organizations believe tens of thousands of people died due to the radiation exposure within just a few years. "Chernobyl" has become a common reference when referring to catastrophic disasters due to manmade errors.

Chernobyl reactor covered by a new containment structure

In 1991, the Ukraine, which was a part of the Soviet Union at the time, became an independent country.

----

1. What was the name of the Soviet nuclear power plant that exploded in 1986?

2. In what Soviet territory (now the name of an independent country) was Chernobyl located?

3. What radioactive element is used to create nuclear energy?

Brain Spark:

1. What was the name of the rebel group that fought a socialist government in Nicaragua and was aided by the United States in the 1980s?

2. In what city was the Stonewall Inn located?

3. At the end of the Cuban Missile Crisis, the Soviet Union agreed to remove missiles from Cuba. In return, the United States agreed to remove missiles from which country?

4. Who became the King of England after King Edward VIII abdicated his throne?

Strange Places and Important Events

THE CHALLENGER

NASA's crowning achievement after the **Apollo** moon program was the development of the reusable **space shuttle**. The shuttle was designed to take off vertically, piggy-backed on large rockets, and land horizontally like a glider plane. The shuttle was quite big; in fact, it could hold a school bus in its cargo bay! NASA began flying the shuttles into space in the early 1980s, and delivered large satellites into orbit.

The **Challenger disaster** was a fatal accident in January 1986. Just 73 seconds after **take-off**, the space shuttle broke apart, leading to the death of all seven astronauts. One of the astronauts was a high school teacher (**Christa McAuliffe**); she would have been the first teacher in space.

The cause of the accident was the failure of an **O-ring** seal on a part of the booster rocket. The O-ring is a circular man-made rubber ring that looks like the letter O. The morning of January 28, 1986, the temperature at the launch site was unusually cold. In fact, it was below freezing (which is quite rare for Florida). This froze the O-ring, and it became **brittle**, leading to the booster rocket exploding.

The space shuttle had no escape system for the astronauts, and it is believed that the astronauts died either when the shuttle lost pressure or when it hit the ocean surface as it fell back down to earth at a speed of over 200 mph.

This was a horrific national disaster that many watched happen live on TV, including many children who were watching while at school. President

Ronald Reagan delivered a speech that night to the nation, remembering those astronauts. The government also launched an investigation into the accident and found that NASA didn't follow a lot of its own safety rules. NASA had to make some big changes before they could start flying astronauts into space again.

Unfortunately, in 2003 the space shuttle **Columbia disintegrated** as it re-entered the atmosphere. All seven astronauts aboard that shuttle mission died. This catastrophic failure was due to a piece of foam striking the **heat shield**, which is designed to protect the shuttle on re-entry from space.

Despite several attempts to improve the safety of the shuttle program, NASA decided to end the program in 2011. NASA had to then rely on the costly Russian space program to get its astronauts into space. By 2020, NASA was able to resume human spaceflight with the help of **SpaceX** (a private commercial rocket company run by **Elon Musk**).

NASA: National Aeronautics and Space Administration.

Brittle: a hard substance that can shatter easily (for example a hard candy made of melted sugar).

Disintegrated: broken up into many small parts.

1. What was the name of the space shuttle that exploded in January 1986?
2. What was the name of the school teacher who was on board the space shuttle Challenger when it exploded?
3. What was the name of the space shuttle that disintegrated in 2003?

Brain Spark:

1. Which Soviet nuclear power plant exploded in 1986?

2. The demonstrations at Kent State occurred as a result of the U.S. invasion of which Southeast Asian country?

3. What is the capital city of Cambodia?

4. Who led the Bolsheviks during the Russian Revolution, and later became the first leader of the newly formed Soviet Union?

BUSH V. GORE

Can you imagine a presidential election that hinges on the outcome of a vote in one Florida county? The 2000 U.S. presidential election was a **nail-biter**, since it was not clear right away who had won the election.

The two major party candidates running for office were **Al Gore** and **George W. Bush**. Al Gore had been the Vice President for eight years under **Bill Clinton**, and was the Democratic candidate. George W. Bush, the son of former U.S President **George H.W. Bush**, was the governor of Texas at the time and the Republican candidate.

The **U.S presidential election** is determined by the **Electoral College**. The 50 U.S. states get a certain number of **electoral votes** depending on how many congressional districts they have (which in turn depends on their population). Most states have a system by which the winner of the statewide election gets all of the electoral votes no matter how close the election is in that state. A candidate needs a total of **271 electoral votes** to win the presidency.

With modern polling technology, the results of an election can be answered within a few hours. However, the vote in Florida was too close to call. It also turned out that the nation was depending on the outcome of the vote in Florida to determine who would win the election, because the other 49 states' electoral votes had not given either of the candidates the needed 271 electoral votes.

The election in Florida was so close that by law the state had to pursue a **machine recount** of all the votes. Within a week of the election, this recount of the votes was completed and showed that George W. Bush was ahead by only 327 votes out of the almost 6 million that were cast. Al Gore had the right to request a **manual recount**, which he pursued in four counties that traditionally vote more Democrat than Republican.

The biggest challenges encountered during the recount involved the **butterfly paper ballots** used in **Palm Beach County**. The butterfly ballot was designed so that voters would select their candidate by punching a hole in the middle of the paper. However, the ballot paper itself was quite confusing, creating the risk that voters would either punch the incorrect hole or punch too many holes. When they started the manual recount, they identified ballots with confusing punch patterns, and polling workers tried to figure out who had been voted for on each of the ballots.

There were **lawsuits** from both the Bush and Gore campaigns, which led to the Florida Supreme Court deciding that the whole state of Florida had to redo a manual recount. More lawsuits were filed, and the case came before the **U.S. Supreme Court**. The U.S. Supreme Court, with a **5-4 decision**, brought an end to the statewide manual recount, effectively handing the presidency to George W. Bush.

Clearly the United States was split quite evenly based on the election results. The media response was similarly split. Many liberal leaning scholars and news sources felt that the decision by the Supreme Court was **partisan**. Since the 2000 election, it has become more and more common for political candidates to pursue legal action at election time.

Nail biter: a situation that creates great anxiety.

Partisan: strongly supports only one political party.

1. Which two candidates battled it out in the U.S. presidential election of 2000?

2. Ultimately, which candidate was declared the winner of the 2000 U.S. presidential election?

3. What controversial ballot design used in Palm Beach County triggered confusion during the 2000 U.S. presidential election?

Brain Spark:

1. What was the name of the school teacher killed in the 1986 explosion of the space shuttle Challenger?
2. Which Marine lieutenant colonel became the face of the Iran-Contra investigation?
3. What Soviet cosmonaut was the first person to enter space?
4. In 1955, who famously refused to adhere to the Jim Crow law that stated she had to give up her bus seat to a white passenger?

2008 FINANCIAL CRISIS

The year 2008 gave us the largest financial disaster since the **Great Depression of 1929**. In fact, it was called the **Great Recession**. Two factors led to this mess. First, banks had become more involved in making risky investments. Second, the U.S. housing **bubble** collapsed.

The housing bubble was primarily triggered by the loosening of rules for **mortgages**. The U.S. government was encouraging home ownership, and banks began offering mortgages to everyone, even families that couldn't afford to pay them back. In fact, banks were so keen on selling mortgages that they made the mortgages cheap and easy to get. They didn't require much of a down payment. They didn't even really need much proof of **income**. Since the mortgages were so attractive, many families agreed to buy homes they could never afford, partially because so many people were convinced that the value of their home would keep on growing.

All of this home buying drove up the value of homes because there were not enough homes to meet all the **demand**.

As the values of homes sky-rocketed, families started to take out loans against the value of their homes (this is called a **cash-out refinance** or a **home equity loan**). They would then spend that money on vacations, renovations, cars, or medical expenses.

Unfortunately, this was not a **sustainable** bubble (and bubbles never last forever, do they?). When families started to run into difficulty paying their monthly mortgage payments, the banks had to take the homes away from them (known as **foreclosure**).

All of a sudden, many foreclosed homes started hitting the market, and this flood of now empty homes were worth less and less. The housing bubble had been popped. The value of homes came crashing down. People were **saddled** with more debt than they could afford. Families lost their jobs and their homes.

Banks were originally meant to protect people's savings (**deposits**), and would generate income and profit by making relatively safe loans. However, in the late 1990s, banks became more and more involved in **investing**. They would often take on very risky loans and investments: the higher the risk, the higher the possibility of profit. If things went wrong, they could lose a lot of money. The banks had invested significant money in supporting the housing bubble, essentially betting that all the mortgages being sold would continue to turn a profit. When people could not afford to pay back their mortgages, the banks' investments failed. As a result, the banks ran out of money which lead to a "**credit freeze**", meaning they could not lend out any more money. This harmed businesses that needed loans to continue to function. Many businesses collapsed, which led to more job losses, which in turn meant more people could not afford their mortgages.

The financial crisis spread to the rest of the world, primarily because U.S. customers generated 33% of the world's consumption in the 2000s (i.e., buying cars, going on vacations, installing new fridges, buying clothes, etc.), despite representing just 4% of the world's population. Every country was impacted in a negative way by this crisis.

Many governments around the world had to work together to try to rebuild trust in banks. They also set up new rules for banks in order to prevent a similar crisis in the future. In addition, the governments were forced to issue "**bail outs**." In the U.S. alone, these bail outs totaled hundreds of billions of dollars just to keep the banks in business.

Bubble: an economic situation where the value of something rapidly increases to an unsustainable level, after which the bubble "pops" and the value rapidly collapses.

Mortgage: a loan provided by a bank to a person for use in buying a home or property. Typically, because buying a home is so expensive, mortgages have significant requirements to prove a person can pay the loan back prior to the bank loaning the money.

Sustainable: capable of being maintained.

Saddled: to burden someone with a large or difficult responsibility.

1. The 2008 financial crisis was largely triggered due to the loosening of rules for giving out what type of home-buying loan?
2. When a bank takes a home away from a homeowner because the owner cannot make their mortgage payments, it is called a _____?
3. What "cold" term describes the refusal of banks to lend money?

Brain Spark:

1. What two presidential candidates faced off in the "nail-biter" 2000 U.S. presidential election?
2. The Chernobyl power plant is located near the town of Pripyat. Can you name the Eastern European country that it belongs to?
3. What was the name of the man who leaked the Pentagon Papers to the New York Times?
4. What was the name of the high school teacher prosecuted for teaching human evolution in 1925?

ABOUT THE AUTHORS

Dr. Michael Harwood graduated from Brown Medical School and is a board-certified Dermatologist. He is also a former Jeopardy! contestant. In addition to spending time with his two boys, he enjoys the piano, golf and writing.

Dr. Adrian Hamburger is a Harvard-trained Anesthesiologist and Pain Specialist, and dedicated father to two teenagers. He loves trivia, skiing, snorkeling, and chasing after his two dogs.

BRAIN SPARK BOOK SERIES

If you enjoyed this book, please consider our other books in the series:

1. Brain Spark – What every kid deserves to know about… Famous People!
2. Brain Spark – Interesting stories and curious facts about… Pop Culture!

Be on the lookout for our next book in the Brain Spark series:

Brain Spark – What every kid needs to know about… Money and Finance!

Made in the USA
Middletown, DE
11 December 2024